C. RUTH TAYLOR
LATE BLOOMER'S EDITION

DESIGN TO WIN ROAD MAP 2

**HOW TO DREAM AGAIN AND SUCCEED
IN LIFE AS YOU GET OLDER**

Extra MILE Innovators
Kingston, Jamaica W.I.

Copyright © 2020 by C. Ruth Taylor
ISBN: 978-1-62676-568-9

ALL RIGHTS RESERVED

Without limiting the rights under copyright reserved above, no part of this publication may be reproduced, stored in or introduced into a retrieval system, or transmitted, in any form, or by any means (electronic, mechanical, photocopying, recording, or otherwise), without the prior contractual or written permission of the copyright owner of this work.

. . . . .

Published by
Extra MILE Innovators
21 Phoenix Avenue,
Kingston 10, Jamaica W.I.
www.extramileja.com
Tele: (1876) 782-9893

Cover Design:
N.D. Author Services [NDAS]
www.NDAuthorServices.com

Editor: Dr. Jean B. Lee

Illustrations: Norman Cooper
normanfcooper@gmail.com

Unless otherwise identified, Scripture quotations are from the New Living Translation, copyright © 1996, 2004, 2007 by Tyndale House Foundation. Used by permission of Tyndale House Publishers, Inc., Carol Stream, Illinois 60188. All rights reserved.

Author Contact

Email ruthtaylor@extramileja.com to book her for speaking engagements, conferences, workshops, Indie publishing advice, mentoring and coaching services.

Free Writing Resource
Download a Free copy of "The Rocket-Writer" from our website
www.extramileja.com.

*To: My mom
and women like Rev. Dr Carla Dunbar and Jo-Ann
Richards-Goffe who taught me by their example I can still win
big as I get older*

FOREWORD

I got an inside view of Cameka Ruth's life when I agreed to house sit or rather cat sit for her when she left the island on one of her missionary journeys. Staying in her house for those few days gave me deeper insight into the real secrets behind Ruth's success.

I can easily describe her as being humble, genuine, honest, focused, enthusiastic, compassionate, minimalist, industrious, loyal, committed to excellence, diligent and determined. All of this however, would never have produced the person we know today without her lifestyle of prayer. Her prayer points are listed in prominent places in her space, and they do not only consist of her own concerns. Ruth is quite likely also praying for you!

I met Ruth shortly after returning from Burkina Faso in 2003, where I served as a missionary with Wycliffe Bible Translators. I observed her and was duly impressed with the consistent progress and a high level of excellence manifested in her life. So impressed I was, that I eventually approached her with the request that she share her success secrets with me ... and she did! (Any lack you see in me is in spite of her advice!)

Having 'hurdled' many life obstacles, financial challenges and broken engagements, Ruth is well-equipped to help guide you through this road map to success, no matter how far along the road you are. The fact that I am almost 20 years her senior, and yet was drawn to her for advice and guidance, should be a clear indicator that her capability and maturity are well beyond her years.

Design to Win Road Map 2: The Late Bloomer's Edition is her 10th publication to date, and she has hit this one way out of the ballpark! (Or as we would say in Jamaica, 'Shi lick it fi six!)

My interest was piqued just by glancing through the table of contents, so I settled down to read. I could not stop reading until I had turned the final page of the manuscript.

From her personal stories, stories of friends, family and acquaintances, to stories of mentors from books and online, to accounts from the Holy Bible, I was hooked. Although her connection with God and commitment to her Christian faith are what drive her, she does not use that to exclude any potential readers. Her message of hope is for everyone.

What truly adds value to this book for me are the acronyms and templates provided to simplify life processes in a practical way for guaranteed improvement and ultimate success. This book is chock full of tools to help you with goal setting, time management, money management and more. Best of all, this transformational book prepares you, the reader, to play a part in bringing transformation to someone else who is waiting for you to "shoot and spring" like the banana tree.

So yes, if you are not yet ready to give up on being your very best self, fulfilling your purpose and being hilariously happy, then grab a pen and paper, shut the rest of the world out for a while, and dig in!

—Jo-Ann Richards-Goffe
Author, Ethnodoxologist
CREW 40:4

Table of Contents

INTRODUCTION 1
Chapter 1: DREAM RESUSCITATION STORIES 3
   1.0 Greatness after 40 5
   1.1 You Can Still Find Love 9
   1.2 You Can Still Get Your Dream Career 14
   1.3 You Can Still Be Used Greatly 20
   1.4 You Can Still Turn Your Life Around 23
Chapter 2 MOVING PAST REGRET, FAILURE AND REJECTION 26
   2.0 Silencing the Voice of Regret 27
   2.1 Overcoming Failure and Rejection 35
Chapter 3: REINVENTION 41
   3.0 A Fresh Start 43
   3.1 Life-Change by Design 50
   3.2 Your Design to Win Framework 53
Chapter 4: A JOURNEY OF SELF-DISCOVERY 57
   4.0 Getting a Picture of Your Past and Present Life 59
   4.1 The Design to Win Survey 62
   4.2 Your Personality and Career Profile 68
Chapter 5: UNDERSTANDING PURPOSE 71
   5.0 What is Your Purpose in Life? 73
   5.1 Purpose Discovery Activities 79

5.2 Envisioning Your Preferred Future 84

CHAPTER 6: CREATING YOUR ACTION PLAN 89

   6.0 Setting Major Life Goals 91

   6.1 Your Macro Design to Win Blueprint 98

   6.2 Tips to Implement Your Design 102

Chapter 7: THE ART OF LIFE HURDLING 105

   7.0 Becoming a Life-Hurdling Champion 107

   7.1 Time Management and Productivity Hacks 111

   7.2 Being Money Smart 121

   7.3 Credit Card Advisory 127

   7.4 Spring Again 133

AFTERWORD: A DREAM REVIVED 137

ACKNOWLEDGMENTS 141

ABOUT THE AUTHOR 143

REFERENCES 145

INTRODUCTION
Delayed Dreams and Age-Old Regrets

It was my 37th birthday and I didn't quite know how to feel although it was my birthday. In fact, I had nothing planned and did not feel like celebrating. Besides, what was there to celebrate? I was only inching closer to 40 and I was still behind on my dreams and behind on my bills! The residue of the sting of failure and regret was still with me despite all my efforts at self-improvement.

What do you do when your dreams have been delayed or derailed as you get older and you are filled with regrets? Should these dreams be discarded? How do you silence the voice of regret and deal with the pain of failure as you grow older? What if you have not achieved greatness in the first half of your life? Is there still reason to hope?

This edition of the *Design to Win Road Map* faces these pertinent questions head on! It has been written to prepare persons 40 years old and over to win and soar to new heights as they get older. Over the years, had it not been for the memory of late bloomers like Zig Ziglar, Joyce Meyer, Brian Tracy, Terri Savelle Foy, Colonel Sanders, Grandma Moses and biblical characters like Sarah, Moses and Abraham, I would have sunken into a serious stupor of unabated despair. Thank God for models of success who achieved greatness beyond the time they were expected to do so.

There are many persons who are battling feelings of regret because they are not where they wanted to be at particular stages of their lives. This feeling cripples them and leads to great despair. I want to help as many people as possible to steer clear of this dragon so that they can go on to achieve their God-given purpose and destinies on their own divinely ordained timetable.

This edition of *Design to Win Road Map* emerged out of my own personal quest for hope and an effort to see dreams from my younger years materialize in my later years. The good news is that my most productive years are still ahead of me at this life stage of generativity or stagnation according to Psychosocial analyst Dr. Erik Erickson. I am determined to produce my life's work and invest in the next generation while soaring to new heights. This is also my prayer for you as you read this book. It is a reminder that **It's not too late to win! Your Dreams are Still Possible!**

This book contains some of my favourite true stories of amazing late bloomers. Their stories (ancient and modern) will mesmerize and inspire you. These true stories represent people across different continents and races who achieved things thought impossible after mid-life and even into their late 90s. It does not matter how old you are, if you are alive and fairly healthy, your dream is still possible! Let's take a dive and let the dream resuscitation and reinvention begin!

Chapter 1:

DREAM RESUSCITATION STORIES

"Never, never, never give up!"
—Sir Winston Churchill

1.0
GREATNESS AFTER 40

Is there a rule that you must attain success or achieve your dreams by the age of 40? And if there is, who made it? Who says big dreams die after age 40? Who says that our most productive years must be in the first half of our lives? As young people, many of us in dreaming of the future often set deadlines to accomplish our most important life goals, especially those relating to marriage, starting our own family, owning our first home and the like, all before the age of 35. If not by then, we certainly want to do so before the dreaded age of 40.

I say dreaded because I'm always disturbed when speakers talk about the 40-year-olds who are still struggling with issues that, according to these speakers, they should have long ago overcome. It seems 40 is the number for maturity based on how they speak, and if at age 40 you have not achieved certain material things or matured to a certain level, then it seems impossible after that! Shame on you for not doing so!

> **Who says that those who achieve big things before 40 are not the exception rather than the norm?**

Who says people like Alexander the Great, Martin Luther King Jnr., Malala Yousafzai, Mark Zuckerberg, Usain Bolt, Bob Marley and the like are not exceptions to the rule? If this is not the norm, then I have good news! It's time to shift your mindset and redesign your life.

Sure enough, I bought the lie for a season that I had to achieve my most important goals before age 40 or I would be a big failure! I felt a deep sense of shame, and became greatly disturbed because although I have achieved much educationally and judge myself to be living a purpose-driven life, there are some ordinary things that have eluded me.

At the time of writing [39 years old] I should have been Dr. Taylor. I should have owned my first home and started a family. But alas! I don't have any of these gains! So, what do you do when your dreams are delayed and many of your friends and schoolmates, and even those younger than you are living your dreams? I have discovered a good coping mechanism: remembering stories of late bloomers. Let's now look at some of them.

You Can Still Have a Child

Their names were Elizabeth and Zechariah, an old priestly couple whose prayers were answered after many decades. Their story is told in the first chapter in the book of Luke in the Bible. As a Christian, I am very fascinated by this story. We are told they (well advanced in years) were good and just people in God's sight. They walked in integrity in God's ways and laws, yet they had sadness. And despite their sadness, they faithfully carried out their priestly duties and never lost their faith. The couple's sadness centred on the wife's infertility. They were childless and both were quite old—well past the normal childbearing years.

1.0 Greatness After 40

One day as the husband Zechariah was in the temple, he got a once in a lifetime opportunity to enter the sacred precincts of the temple and while a large crowd gathered outside, Zecharias had an angelic encounter. An angel visited him and told him that his wife would become pregnant and have a son who would become a great man. Of course, like any normal person, Zechariah was in disbelief. He told the angel this was impossible. "This is hard to believe," he said. "I am an old man and my wife is well past the normal age for women to have children" (Luke 1:18).

In response to his unbelief the angel took away his ability to speak. This ability to speak would only return at the birth of his son. While this supernatural encounter took place, the crowd was concerned because it was not normal for the priest to be delayed so long. When at last Zecharias came out, he could only make motions with his hand. The crowd realized he must have seen some vision.

Suffice it to say, shortly after returning home, his wife became pregnant much to her amazement! So much so, that she avoided public appearance for five months. But what I find remarkable is what his wife, Elizabeth said. In that time and still today in certain parts of the world, women who do not bear children are a sign of disgrace. Elizabeth said, "I have lived with the disgrace of being barren all these years. Now God has looked on me with favour. When I go out in public with my baby, I will not be disgraced any longer" (Luke 1: 25). Eventually she gave birth to a son, named John, the renowned "John the Baptist" who became a very great man just as the angel said. Elizabeth and Zechariah's story holds many truths for us including the following:

1. It is still possible for our delayed dreams to materialize.

2. Miracles still happen.

3. Prayers still get heard after many years.

4. You don't have to lose your faith because your dreams do not materialize.

5. You can love and serve God faithfully and still have sadness because of unmet desires.

This couple's story truly gives me hope that what may appear to be unfulfilled dreams are not dreams denied. It's still possible to live our dreams even in our old age. Let's now look to some contemporary examples.

1.1
YOU CAN STILL FIND LOVE

It was Mothers' Day 2015, and as usual, I decided to give my mother a special treat. There were several announcements on the radio and on social media about a Mothers' Day treat at Hope Gardens, one of the national parks in Jamaica. I asked Mom if she would like to go. Mom responded in the affirmative and we made our plans to go and have a nice picnic and enjoy all that the organizers of the event had to offer. To our surprise, there was also an outside radio broadcast and Mom got a chance to be interviewed by one of the journalists. We also engaged in a mini spending spree and later decided to relax on the lush green grass at Hope Gardens.

After a little search, we found an appropriate spot to spread our towels, lie on the grass, engage in small talk and enjoy the sights and scenes of the afternoon. While lying on the grass, I saw an elderly couple enjoying themselves and I motioned to my Mom to follow my gaze. I was thoroughly fascinated by their love play and thought, "Wow, their love has truly not gone cold after so many years!" For some reason, I could not take my eyes off them and I told my mother to join me in a little investigation to find out the secret of their love. I was drawn to this couple without knowing why and I could tell they were deeply in love with each other.

My mother and I made our way over to the couple and introduced ourselves. We told them how we were admiring them from a distance and wanted to meet them in person. The couple told us a story that is forever etched in my heart as a single woman. It was fascinating! Mr. and Mrs. Reid were both in their late sixties. They were not a couple whose love had blossomed like fine wine. They were newlyweds! They were newlyweds at their age!

While courting, Mr. and Mrs. Reid referred to themselves as 'old virgins,' although this was Mrs. Reid's third marriage and the first for Mr. Reid. They were both dedicated Christians and during their courtship, Mrs. Reid determined in her heart that she did not want her relationship to be what she referred to as 'fleshy love.' This meant she did not want her relationship to be focused on the physical expressions of love. It was a fascinating story! She told us that she and Mr. Reid refrained from sexual intercourse until the night of their wedding. They had followed an ancient path even at their age, stage and past experiences. They are now very happy for all to see!

Mr. Reid described his days prior to coming to the Christian faith as such; "I was a wild man; a womanizer." During that time, he fathered five children out of wedlock. Sometime later, he became a Christian and after several failed attempts at getting married, he told God to choose a wife for him. Although he was sexually active prior to becoming a Christian, he was able to abstain from sex for many years after becoming a Christian. Again, this shows that change is possible!

According to Mr. Reid, God chose Mrs. Reid to be his wife at the age of 66! His story reaffirms to me that it is never too late to go in the right direction. Therefore, for those who desire to walk the path of sexual purity, please note this is not a mission impossible but a mission possible. For those over 60 who have never been married, it's still possible to love again and get married.

1.1 You Can Still Find Love

After meeting this couple, I found other stories of those who found love late and these stories were much closer to home. One case really blew my mind. I met a Jamaican lady whose mother married for the first time at 50 years old and after her husband died, she remarried at 85 years old and died at 95 years of age!

Marrying Late in the MCAJ

This bug of marrying late has really hit the Missionary Church Association (MCAJ) like a breath of fresh air. I'll begin with my friend Jo-Ann Richards Goffe, a renowned ethnodoxologist in Jamaica and a former Missionary with Wycliffe Bible Translators Caribbean. She wrote the foreword for this book. She is also a teacher by profession and founder of CREW 40:4, a non-profit organization that specializes in advocating for and developing Culturally Relevant Expressions of Worship (CREW). Jo-Ann shares in her book, "Godincidences" that in her younger years she had been engaged to be married but that relationship did not work out. It also appeared to onlookers that perhaps Jo-Ann would remain single for the rest of her life.

However, this was not to be the case. At the age of 51, she finally got married. I was privileged to have attended this musical wedding fiesta and watched a glowing bride and her groom take their marriage vows. Her example also stands as a vivid reminder that you can love again even if you had a failed engagement previously. This is particularly inspiring for me since I have had two failed engagements. Since then, I have met at least three Jamaicans (3 males and one female) who've gone on to marry after a failed engagement.

Three other couples whom I personally know have married late since 2015. My friend Grace-Ann Taylor-Meyers, got married at age 49, after many failed attempts at relationships including one engagement. Her story is somewhat like that of Ruth in the Old Testament book, as she moved from the city to rural Jamaica to care for her aging parents. She met and married a missionary from another race and culture. They live and operate a ministry in Spicy Grove, St. Mary, "Bringing hope and the love of Christ to children, youth and their families." Following their lead too, is one of my great friends and fellow missionary to Cuba for many years, Claudette Distant-Lindo, who in her sixties tied the knot in 2016.

Not to be left out is the reinvention story and late marriage of one of my former pastors, Rev. Mark Dawes. He was a journalist for 18 years who changed careers to become a pastor. Within a few years of this career change, when he was 47 years old, he tied the knot with a lawyer who was also in her forties. This was the first marriage for both of them. For a Christian professional woman like me, who still has a dream of getting married, these are truly models of inspiration and hope. I believe their stories are also models for you.

Marrying into Royalty

Early in 2018, the whole world began once again to believe fairy tales do come true when Prince Harry of England married Meghan Markle, an American who was not of royal lineage. Not only was she not of royal lineage, but she was also a divorcee and a bi-racial woman whose mother is black and whose father is Caucasian. Meghan is an actress as well as a feminist activist. Their wedding was a spectacular event and a great display of unity, hope and love.

Similarly, on the African continent, another feminist activist, female broadcaster and journalist extraordinaire, Gifty Anti, married a chief (an African king). However, unlike Prince Harry and Meghan Markle, a young couple in their thirties, Gifty Anty married in her forties at the age of 45, two years prior to the British royals in 2016.

1.1 You Can Still Find Love

According to Ghana Nation news, Chief of Edumasa, Nana Ansah Kwao says marrying ace broadcaster Gifty Anti now known as Awo Dansoa is a dream come true. "I'm very happy to have Gifty Anti as a wife. In fact, marrying her is a dream come true for me because I now have a wife after my own heart," he said. Nana Ansah Kwao explained that his wife is a woman who believes in the best and "I really love that about her and that even drew me closer to her more…"To have a woman is a very good thing and even the Bible confirms it and I'm so happy to be the man for Awo Dansoa."

On her part, the latest royal bride and TV icon, Gifty Anti, now Awo Dansoa, said she feels honoured to be married to Edumasa chief Nana Ansah Kwao. She cannot hide her excitement because her marriage has lifted her above all the rude comments she has endured over the years. Gifty Anti was grateful to her in-laws for accepting her with all the flaws and for honouring the Anti family adding that "I'm ready to learn how to be the wife of a chief."

This is Gifty Anti's first marriage and what makes her story even more phenomenal is that, not only did she become royalty, but she gave birth to her first child at age 47. If ever there was a story that dreams still come true in our 21st Century, this sure is one. In fact, all these contemporary stories are a reminder that dreams do come true in our later years. If you still desire a family or dream of finding love, these stories from Africa to Europe to the Caribbean should certainly give you hope. It's not too late to love and start your own family!

1.2
YOU CAN STILL GET YOUR DREAM CAREER

The pursuit of a dream is often like an odyssey with its many twists and turns. It is very much like growing strong trees. Strong trees do not grow overnight. They have weathered many storms and today they stand tall, having withstood the tests of life. Strong trees are a reminder that no matter how bad it is or how bad it gets; we should rise above adversities and stand tall.

Nurse Davy-Gordon is a strong tree that has weathered many storms. Her story is that of a Jamaican woman who refused to give up on her childhood dream of becoming a registered nurse despite a 37-year delay. Her story is very endearing to me because she is my mother and I have had a front-row view of watching this late bloomer soar from one dimension to another.

How many of you remember as a child being asked: "What do you want to be when you grow up?" Well, my Mom remembers that at eight all she wanted was to become a Registered Nurse and graduate from the University of the West Indies, but a major obstacle stood between her and her dream—poverty. Life was hard. She was the fifth of nine children raised

1.2 You Can Still Get Your Dream Career

by a single mother in a poor rural agricultural district in St. Mary.

Her family was so poor that people in the district expected very little of them. Some community members said she would never amount to anything good. Mom took these words to heart and was determined to prove them wrong.

Educational Challenges and the Dream

As a child, Mom's intelligence was clear and she paid careful attention in school. She showed grit and tenacity and commitment to education. Despite not having lunch on many school days, she was not be deterred from attending school and she worked hard. During her school years, my grandmother, a single parent, worked on a banana plantation and of course, that meant she did not earn enough to send her nine children to school all at the same time.

When most children opted to stay home from school on Fridays, which was the norm in Mom's hometown, Mom ensured she didn't because Friday was the day when the principal would ask current affairs questions during devotion. If you got the questions right, you would win books, pencils and other things. That was one way she got things for school. Eventually, her hard work paid off, and she won a place at a newly established high school, Jose Marti Technical, but once again, poverty prevented her from seizing this opportunity.

Disappointed but determined, Mom remained at Mount Angus All-Age School and eventually gained a place at another school: Guys Hill Secondary. And since my grandmother still could not afford it, Mom became resourceful and began implementing measures to seize the opportunity. She asked her neighbour for help to make her uniform (the neighbour's child was attending the institution). Her entrepreneurial skills then surfaced as she would sell coconut oil and oranges to earn money to send herself to school, but it was still not enough.

The distance to travel to school began to take its toll because unlike Mount Angus, Guy's Hill was nine miles away and if she missed the bus or could not find the money to pay the fare, she would have to walk to school. Fortunately, when she was in grade eight, the principal allowed her to live at her home and it made life easier.

However, this good fortune did not immediately propel Mom any step closer to achieving her dream. Misfortune presented herself through peer pressure and at 17, Mom found herself socially embarrassed and dejected. She became pregnant with me, her first child.

After giving birth to me, Mom did whatever she could to make ends meet. She went back to grating coconuts to make coconut oil and fortunately received some help from my paternal grandmother who encouraged her to go to the city so she could have a better life. Thus, at two, we were separated when Mom left St. Mary to improve her life. She left me in the care of my paternal family in another parish.

Pregnancies and the Pursuit of a Better Life

Despite the setback and the disruption of education, with this blessing, her hope of achieving her dream was renewed. Mom moved to the city of Kingston in search of a better life, and this move landed her in the Inner City of Olympic Gardens. Life in Kingston was difficult because Mom was unskilled and securing a good and stable job was challenging.

Mom was teachable and well-mannered. These traits brought more blessings. She eventually found a home with some kind strangers who encouraged and helped her to get a fresh start.

1.2 You Can Still Get Your Dream Career

Five years later, my sister was born and a year after came my brother. This time there were no relatives to help. With three children, life was even more challenging. Mom was determined to overcome her circumstances, and over the next thirteen years held several odd jobs. She worked in the garment factories and quickly learned the skill of a seamstress.

Once more, Mom employed her entrepreneurial skills by selling goods and produce at Coronation Market. She sold juices at the gate of primary schools and at her home. Eventually she got married and became a practical nurse.

At this juncture, all her efforts and investment were focused on caring for and educating her three children, who were all now living with her in Olympic Gardens. In due course, Mom gained steady employment at the Kingston Public Hospital (KPH) as a Ward Assistant for ten years, and during this period, the dream lay dormant.

The Turning Point

One fateful afternoon, at a Parent-Teachers' Meeting at my high school, Meadowbrook High, a presenter challenged the parents to not only invest in their children, but also themselves and not give up on their dreams. The speaker said that parents should never use their children as an excuse to not make their lives better. They must never blame their children for not being able to achieve their personal dreams, but should work simultaneously to improve themselves. Mom took to heart what the presenter said and, at 37, decided to once again pursue her childhood dream of becoming a Registered Nurse.

This pursuit was no easy feat because Mom had none of the qualifying subjects. The matriculation requirement was five Caribbean Examination Council (CXC) subjects including Mathematics and English.

Mom was determined to succeed this time. While she worked, she attended evening classes for three of the subjects and taught herself two of them. Mathematics and English were very challenging. After four attempts, she passed Math and after approximately seven attempts, she passed English. Her hard work and determination finally paid off, and she enrolled in Brown's Town Community College to pursue a Bachelor of Science in Nursing at 42.

Finally, at the age of 45, Mom's childhood dream had become a reality!

Success at Last

At this point, we were adults and Mom was able to relocate to St. Ann to facilitate her studies. Fortunately for Mom, the community college had a partnership with the University of the West Indies. Hers was the second batch pursuing a nursing degree over a three-year period. Previously, nurses after three years would graduate with a diploma only but God again smiled upon her.

Although life as a student was challenging those three years, with faith in God, a good attitude and hard work, Mom graduated with second class honours as a Registered Nurse with a Bachelor of Science in Nursing! You should have seen how Mom and my grandmother proudly strutted the campus of the University of the West Indies to celebrate!

She had finally defied the odds and silenced the naysayers, but her educational pursuits did not end there. Within three years Mom improved on her qualifications by specializing in Nephrology and caring for patients with End Stage Renal failure. By age 50, Mom had not only achieved her childhood dream career, but she had purchased a home and ensured the

1.2 You Can Still Get Your Dream Career

success of her three children who by then all had careers. I became an educator, author and speaker; my sister became a Registered Nurse and my brother became self-employed as an auto-electrician.

When Mom turned 50, we honoured her publicly for her sacrifice and persistence, which had paid off tremendously. And that was not all. At 53, she returned to school to study midwifery and at age 55, she again returned to school to become a Nurse Manager. Today, she is not only a Registered Nurse with a degree but one who is also a midwife and one who specializes in nephrology. She is a "Sister" (a 'boss nurse' in charge of a ward).

In 2019, at age 56, her contribution to nursing was recognized and they gave her an award by the Nursing Association in Jamaica for 24 years of dedicated service to the profession.

Mom's story is already inspiring others to go after their dreams. Recently, a member of our church told me that because of my Mom's story (she read it in my book *When Trees Talk*), she went back to school to get two CXC subjects as part of her own pursuit to do her undergraduate degree.

Is there a dream in your heart that is still worth pursuing? Let my Mom's 37 years of chasing her dream push you to achieve yours. It's not too late! Don't ever give up!

Note: In the first printed story in *When Trees Talk*, I got the timeline wrong. Mom corrected me in this updated version. She graduated at age 45.

1.3
YOU CAN STILL BE USED GREATLY

Another of my favourite true stories from the Bible is the story of Ruth and Naomi. In fact, this led me to adopt the name Ruth. However, my focus will be on Naomi to inspire us to revive our dreams. Naomi was an influential woman who was married and had two sons. She resided in Bethlehem of Judah for many years and then a famine broke out. In order to spare their lives, the family decided to migrate to a country called Moab.

While in Moab, Naomi's life turned upside down. In her words God, gave her "bitter pills and hard blows." Shortly after moving to Moab, her husband died and sometime after, her two sons married Moabite women. However, things took a turn for the worse. Within 10 years she lost both of her sons and, as might be expected, Naomi, whose name meant pleasant, became a bitter woman.

In her state of bitterness and sadness, she heard the economy of Bethlehem was doing better and she decided to return home. Her two daughters-in-law decided to accompany her and Naomi did her best to dissuade them repeatedly. Eventually, one of them yielded to her dissuasion. What struck me in Naomi's argument is her hopelessness regarding her age. She felt she was too old to be of any use. She told them she was poor and could not have any more children. It would be foolish for them to wait

1.3 You Can Still Be Used Greatly

for her to have children whom they could marry again. Her life was too bleak for them to share in it.

Nevertheless, the daughter-in-law named Ruth refused to listen. She decided to leave her people and cling to Naomi to take care of her forever and to serve Naomi's God. Naomi was very surprised. In that time, widows without sons would be destitute and this young widow was willing to leave her home country to live in a hostile country just to take care of her mother-in-law! This was unheard of then and still today!

Notwithstanding, God was not through with Naomi. She was old but not useless. To cut a long story short, Naomi's age-old wisdom and associations became beneficial to Ruth. Naomi became a match-maker and Ruth ended up marrying one of her rich relatives named Boaz. They then went from poverty to plenty but that's not all. Naomi and Ruth became matriarchs of a family that changed the nation of Israel and the world. Ruth gave birth to a son whose grandson became the second king in Israel. He united the tribes in his country and defeated their enemies. That king's name is immortalized. He is the king that defeated a giant named Goliath. His name is David! And from David's lineage came the greatest king, the Messiah of Israel and the saviour of the world —Jesus, the Christ.

Naomi's story along with the others, teach us several lessons to revive our dreams. Some of these are as follows:

1. **You are not too old to be used greatly.** Did not one of England's greatest Prime Ministers, Sir Winston Churchill, become Prime Minister at age 70? Did not God call Abraham for the greatest mission of his life at age 75? Didn't he conceive his promised child at age 100, remarry and have six more children with his second wife? Was not Moses called at 80 to lead one of the greatest acts of liberation in history?

2. **You can achieve at any age. Age is just a number**: Many people have gone on to do great things after age 50. Some of these include: Gladys Burrill, who earned the Guinness Book of World Records as the oldest female to complete a marathon. At age 92, she finished the race, which took place in Honolulu in nine hours, 53 minutes and 16 seconds!

   Didn't Grandma Moses, one of the greatest painters, begin her career at age 76? Grandma Moses, the spry, indomitable "genuine American primitive" who became one of the country's most famous painters turned out her first painting at the age of 76. She took up painting because arthritis had crippled her hands so that she no longer could embroider. Three years later, her art was hanging at the Museum of Modern Art in New York.

   In my country, most of those who receive the greatest national honours on Heroes Day are usually over 50 years of age. One of the awardees was my pastor, Rev. Rennard White, who received an Order of Distinction from the government of Jamaica in October 2018, at the age of 70. Did not Nelson Mandela become the first black president of South Africa at age 77?

> **Don't write yourself off because you are old or have had a series of misfortunes. The tide can still turn.**

1.4
YOU CAN STILL TURN YOUR LIFE AROUND

Winning after Retirement

This inspiring story never fails to give me hope. This is his story as written by Rachel Denison on her blog. Colonel Sanders was born in 1890 in Henryville, IN. When he was six years old, his father passed away leaving Sanders to cook and care for his siblings. In seventh grade, he dropped out of school and left home to go to work as a farmhand. At 16, he faked his age to enlist in the United States army. After being honourably discharged a year later, he got hired by the railway as a labourer.

However, he got fired for fighting with a co-worker. While he worked for the railway, he studied law until he ruined his legal career by getting into another fight. This forced Sanders to move back in with his Mom and get a job selling life insurance. And guess what? He got fired for insubordination. But this guy wouldn't give up.

In 1920, he founded a ferry boat company. Later, he tried cashing in his ferry boat business to create a lamp manufacturing company, only to find out that another company already sold a better version of his lamp. It wasn't until age 40 that he began selling chicken dishes in a service station. As he began to advertise his food, an argument with a competitor resulted in a deadly shootout. Four years later, he bought a motel which burned to the ground along with his restaurant. He rebuilt a new motel until World War II forced him to close it down.

Following the war, he tried to franchise his restaurant. His recipe was rejected 1,009 times before anyone accepted it. Sander's "secret recipe" was coined "Kentucky Fried Chicken", and quickly became a hit. However, the booming restaurant was crippled when an interstate opened nearby, so Sanders sold it and pursued his dream of spreading KFC franchises and hiring KFC workers all across the country.

After years of failures and misfortunes, Sanders finally hit it big. KFC expanded internationally and he sold the company for two million dollars ($15.3 million today). Even today, Sanders remains central in KFC's branding and his face still appears in their logo. His goatee, white suit and western string tie continue to symbolize delicious country fried chicken all over the world. At age 90, Sanders passed away from pneumonia. At that time, there were around 6,000 KFC locations in 48 countries. By 2013, there were an estimated 18,000 KFC locations in 118 countries! If you're overwhelmed by rejection or discouraged by setbacks, remember the story of Colonel Harland Sanders. Sanders wouldn't let anything or anyone defeat him.

Four (4) International Speakers

The final set of stories relates to my industry. These four individuals always inspire me because they all began to turn their lives around at my age or a little after. When despair threatens, I usually say, "Joyce Meyer started her ministry at age 40. Look at her today! Terri Savelle Foy and Brian Tracy

1.4 You Can Turn Your Life Around

turned their lives around at age 38 and look at them today. Zig Ziglar got his big break at age 40 and look at his impact years later!"

Joyce Meyer is one of the world's leading Christian female ministers. She has one of the largest ministries in the world despite her early challenges. She came from a life of sexual abuse by her father that left her a deeply troubled woman. She had a divorce and later remarried. Now she is the author of over 60 books and has worldwide influence.

Terri Savelle Foy is the author of several books and the daughter of Jerry Savelle. She now has her own ministry. She, too, had a troubled past, filled with insecurities and fear as well as a voice completely opposite to Joyce Meyer's deep voice. Hers is like a little child and yet her influence has spread to continents through her books and conferences.

Zig Ziglar was one of the world's greatest motivational Christian speakers. He authored several books and his legacy lives on, although he has died. Brian Tracy is a Canadian-American motivational public speaker and self-development author. He is the author of over seventy books that have been translated into dozens of languages. He came from a labouring background and did not do well in high school. Today (2019) he is well-known and at age 75 still gets many speaking engagements. He has helped many Fortune 500 companies over the years and his books are widely used.

Dream Revival Insights

1. It's not too late to get it right and go after your dreams.

2. Even if you start late, you can still leave a lasting legacy.

3. Despite your history of failure, abuse and setbacks, you can still win!

Chapter 2
MOVING PAST REGRET, FAILURE AND REJECTION

Allow the breeze that brought a maize plant down to strengthen it.
—African Proverb

"Forget regret or life is yours to miss."
—Jonathan Larson

2.0
SILENCING THE VOICE OF REGRET

The voice of regret often comes after failure or a missed opportunity, echoed by the word, "if only" or "I should have already." I know this voice very well! It has been the source of much pain as I edge closer to 40. If only I had been wiser, I would not have entered those relationships. If only I had known better, I would not have gone into credit card debt. If only I knew then what I know now? ...And the list of if onlys, only grows.

What are your regrets? How do you overcome these regrets? If we fail to overcome these regrets we will not move forward. Regret keeps us trapped in the past and causes us to miss the opportunities of the present. Regret causes us to lose sight of the lessons learnt and miss the blessings of the present. To overcome it, we have to initially say like the Apostle Paul in the Bible, "...forgetting what lies behind, I press for the mark of the prize..." (Philippians 3:14). But just how do we forget the past and forge ahead?

One night, when the voice of regret was screaming loudly in my head and leading me into the abyss of despair, I posted a question on Facebook "How does one overcome the feeling or regret/failure as you grow older?" The responses from my friends were insightful. I compiled some of them and created some tips to overcome regret as you grow older.

Tips to Overcome Regret

1. *Understand your psychosocial stage of development* — Nordia McIntosh-Vassell

What is your stage of development? Awareness of it can give insight to alleviate the feeling of regret. Some of my regrets and failure centred around relationships, loneliness and isolation. Intimacy versus isolation is the sixth stage of Erik Erikson's theory of psychosocial development. This stage takes place during young adulthood between the ages of approximately 18 and 40 years. During this period, the major conflict centres on forming intimate, loving relationships with other people. During this period, we begin to share our-selves more intimately with others.

We explore relationships leading toward longer-term commitments with someone other than a family member. Successful completion of this stage can result in happy relationships and a sense of commitment, safety, and care within a relationship. Avoiding intimacy, fearing commitment and relationships can lead to isolation, loneliness, and sometimes depression. Success in this stage will lead to the virtue of love…

2. *Introspect and count your blessings* – Nordia McIntosh Vassell

Help me here: the FEELING right?…Introspection is the first step then identify the elements from the introspection that ONE FEELS…using a guide (Biblical, Successful Plan

2.0 Silencing the Voice of Regret

List from renowned authors etc.) begin to literally COUNT, as it were, the blessings, the successes etc. and then examine the parts of those areas that cause one to think that they have failed...I promise you that more times than not the FEELING is as a result of things that ONE had NO CONTROL OF and/or comparing self to others (hard to admit)...

Examining feelings can be tricky because we tie them up with results of a task; ...it is important to separate the two and it must be done with someone else...accountability partner etc... Then there is the issue of gender and how we process these things as women and men, teen boy vs teen girl etc.

3. *Perspective and repositioning* – Nickell Bailey

I think a person's view of failure is linked to the score we give ourselves based on our personal goal achievements divided by the score others give us for what they expect us to achieve. It sometimes leaves us in a deficit. That is a lot to carry. I think one way to get over that feeling is to reposition. It doesn't mean that you have to give up all your dreams and aspirations but find new ways of creating a life of meaning and purpose. For example, for a family member of mine, she adopted her son after waiting to have a child in her marriage for years. Her friend who is single and waiting for years also adopted a child and both kids are now college age.

My grandmother, born 1919, loved Bible study but could not read. She got frustrated and joined JAMAL (Jamaica Foundation for Lifelong Learning) at a ripe old age and learned to read the Bible as her item at rally lol. Reposition. I wanted to be a lawyer and wanted to go to sixth form but I couldn't afford it. I went into Counselling and Educational Psychology while working and raising a family and that field has certainly embraced me.

I still plan to do Law, way down the road, just as a 'what the heck'. One day I shared that sixth form story with one of my young Interns and it set her free because she was carrying that burden of running into friends who were finished with college, and she was still working and going to school because of finances.

4. *View yourself in God's eyes...Be mindful of "Due Season"* – Vaughn Tucker

Keep looking at who you are in Christ. I cannot overemphasize that there is a danger in looking at oneself too much; this will lead to a dangerous cycle of depression and all sorts of oppression... Now as for our past, maybe we have wasted opportunities; the answer is still Jesus. God does not treat us according to our past, but who we are in Christ. There are also examples in the Bible of people God used who felt unworthy.

Moses looked like a failure until the burning bush. He was 40 years old when he went into the wilderness, spent another 40 in the wilderness, which is 80 years. He had a dream, a vision, but saw no fruit. I wonder what his thought process was during his waiting period, but he kept busy. God was training him.

Maybe if we don't make the splash we dream of, it is because we are being trained. So, I say to Ruth Taylor, here is something practical: keep busy serving in humility and in due season you will be lifted up. There is something called due season...

2.0 Silencing the Voice of Regret

Nordia chimed in and said in relation to Vaughn's response, "stay in the process and the product will be out of this world."

5. *Accept choices and be at peace with them* – Cynthia Pearson

    The regrets won't vanish. We gradually learn to accept the choices we made and be at peace with some of them.

6. *Change and seek forgiveness* – Vena Morgan

    If you have regrets in relation to what you may have done wrong, that's where repentance comes in. Repentance and forgiveness… Go before God truthfully and humbly. Ask God to heal and make you whole. Repentance and forgiveness… His grace is sufficient.

7. *Think of lessons learned* – Jamie Johnson

    I think one way to overcome the feeling of regret is to look at the lessons learned from the situation that is causing you pain or sadness. When I am regretting something, I am either feeling sad, hurt or angry…pretty much mainly negative emotions. I personally have never heard of someone regretting something that gave them a positive feeling. I would, therefore, try to see what lessons I learned from the situation and then work on focusing on the benefits of the situation rather than focusing on the negatives. Whatever we feed our mind is whatever will grow and fester.

    Regret, I think also comes with what we think that we missed out on…that job offer that we turned down, or that trip never taken. We don't know what could have happened. It could have been the best or worst thing ever. Again, it might be best to focus on our lessons learned.

I went to Japan and failed. I came back labelling myself as a failure. I often used to wonder what if I stayed. I call myself foolish for my decision to come home. But in the end, what have I gained? I am now an entrepreneur. I have seen the birth of three nieces. I am helping my Mom with my grandma. I was here when my brother bought his house. These are precious things to me. I was able to connect with my uncle and now he helps my Mom out with grandma.

Sure, during the time back, I made more mistakes lol. I am happy that I went. And had I not gone I would have learned to find a way to be happy as well. I think the very best way to overcome regret is to first understand why we are regretful and what emotions are attached to it, and then look for all of the positives that came from the situation and only focus on those.

As said before, their responses were insightful and helpful. I will add three more things that help me to silence the voice of regret and in the next chapter tell you how the game of dominoes can teach us how to handle failure and rejection.

8. Give yourself a reset button.

Whenever I fail or feel regret, I press the reset button mentally. Psychologically, this gives me a fresh start. I say to myself that each day is a new day and I am starting afresh today. The past does not count. The future is not here and all I have is today. Let me live in a new way today.

I once heard, author and motivational speaker, Lisa Nichols say, "I give myself a thousand resets." I have adopted this.

2.0 Silencing the Voice of Regret

Besides, God's mercies are new every day and all we truly have is today. Crying over the past will not change it. It's spilled milk. What matters now are the actions I take today towards a better future.

9. *Just get there.*

I adopted this as a new liberating thought in recent times. It does not matter if you get there early or late, what matters is getting there or die trying to get there. When you arrive at your goal, people seldom remember your struggles or ask how long it took. When they meet you, they are only seeing you as you are today. No wonder it is said, "They see your glory but not your story." As long as you are breathing, it's still possible to get there, to a better destination and to do better than you did yesterday.

10. *The gift of regret*

In 2019, I listened to a podcast with author, leadership expert and former head of Thomas Nelson Publishers, Michael Hyatt. In that podcast, he said, "What if regret were a feature and not a bug? He said a psychology professor at the University of Michigan, Janet Lanman, identified several benefits of regret. Three of which include the following:

    a. *Instruction*: Regret is a form of instruction. Reflecting on our missed steps is critical to avoiding those missteps in the future.

    b. *Motivation to change:* Regret not only tells us that something is wrong but it forces us to do something about it.

c. *Integrity*: Regret can be a moral compass that lets us know when we have veered off course.

Other researchers have also found that feelings of dissatisfaction drive us to correct and fix what is wrong. Regret is the fuel for opportunity and the springboard to a better future. I can definitely relate to these tips and findings. It is my regrets that have fuelled my ministry to empower others, especially youths to get it right early.

It is my regrets that forced me to find solutions to my problems. It is my regrets that have now caused me to realize the dangers of fear and unbelief. It is my regrets that forced me to embrace my destiny and become determined to conquer fear and walk in my greatness. It is time you silence the voice of regret by finding the gift in it. It's time to start planning for the future but before we do, let us deal with two siblings of regret: *failure* and *rejection*.

2.1
OVERCOMING FAILURE AND REJECTION

One of our favourite pastimes in Jamaica is playing a game of dominoes. This is a board game that men especially love to play, and on weekends, we can find Jamaican men all around the island playing a game of dominoes. Children also have a love for dominoes, especially the young boys. I believe this is something we can capitalize on in a number of ways. My friend, Rev. Carla Dunbar, has capitalized on men's love for dominoes and has used it in her work of evangelism to lead men to faith in Jesus Christ. I, too, have now found a way to use dominoes: to teach youths and adults how to handle rejection and failure.

Experiences of rejection and failure—regardless of the context or reason—are very painful. I recently learnt that rejection activates the same pain centre in the body as being physically wounded. This pain is both emotional and physical, and I have experienced both. Relational rejections hurt like a deep knife wound in the heart, especially when the relational ties are strong. When a relationship fails, it is damaging. Divorce, for example, is an extremely painful experience that can have prolonged negative effects for years. Regardless of the reason for rejection or failure, the game of dominoes can help us to get over these hurdles.

When Dominoes Talk

I encourage you to research the game of dominoes and its rules if you are unfamiliar with dominoes. Suffice it to say, in its simplest form, the game is about matching pieces of tiles with numbers. A domino is any of 28 small oblong pieces marked with 0–6 pips in each half. The game usually has four players, who each select (draw) seven random domino tiles. Each player then takes turns to match the pieces. The player who finishes his hand first, wins. If, however, the game is blocked, meaning there are no more matches, the player with the lowest count wins. You would add all the pips of your remaining dominoes to get your count.

There are times in the game when a player has no matching pieces and when it's his turn to play; the player will exclaim: "Pass!" It's in a sense a game of chance. Players can pass several times but eventually their time to play will come again. It's important to remember that when a player selects his seven pieces of dominoes that he does not see the numbers on the tiles. Thus, he cannot control the tile selection. Although a player can lose a match that does not mean that he will lose the game as it is usually six rounds. If he continues playing, he will learn from his mistakes and may even eventually win the game.

These facts are important if we are to learn how to handle rejection and failure from a game of dominoes. Below are some insights from the game to help us to overcome rejection and failure.

2.1 Overcoming Failure and Rejection

1. *See Rejection/Failure as a "Pass" or Bad Fit.*

In the game of dominoes, when you "pass" it simply means the domino does not fit because there is no matching piece. When a relationship ends, try to see it as just that. It simply was not a match or it was a bad fit. For one reason or another, it required a "pass." When you fail to get the promotion or get repeatedly rejected in your job-hunting, bear in mind the game of dominoes. See it as a "pass." Remember, a pass does not mean that a player can never play again. Even if it occurs repeatedly, eventually the player's match comes and he can play.

Say to yourself: "Eventually my match will come. Eventually, I will get it right. Eventually, I will find the right fit." This particular relationship/situation may not have worked, but who says the game is over? Your match may still be out there and you may still get it right.

2. *See Rejection / Failure as a Chance to Improve*

In the game of dominoes, one must learn to read the game. When you can read the game well, you have a better chance of winning. When you are rejected or have failed, you should see it as a chance to learn to improve yourself. If you learn a lesson because of it, that is a blessing. Author and pastor, Dr. Dharius Daniels, once said, "Rejection is a blessing when you find the lesson in it." My relational rejections and failures have taught me much about myself; I now have a better sense of self-worth. I am actually making wiser decisions as a result. I am now studying and spending time with those who are doing well relationally so that I can do better next time. I am learning to read the game of relationships and studying to improve my game.

3. *See Failure or Rejection as Redirection.*

It could be that you are not good at dominoes but better at chess. The game has to end at some point. Then the players leave and find something else to do. The failure could be a redirection to the right path or your divine destiny. My failed relationships were clear redirection for greater things. Sometimes when it does not work, move on to something else or someone else.

4. *Don't Give Up—You Can Still Win*

Some of my students have learnt over the years that it is important to keep a level head when you "pass" or lose a round of dominoes because you can still win the game. The first time one of my students experienced this in the game it was exciting to see and it was a powerful teaching moment. Then it happened to my niece after we were leading her by four rounds.

Both my niece and my student became upset at first when they had multiple passes and could not win a game. My student was angry and almost stopped the game. My niece cried and almost quit. I encouraged them to keep playing and eventually, both won. The lesson in staying in the game helped my niece to handle losing a spelling bee championship. She did not cry and was graceful in defeat. If you have been failing and getting rejected, I know it is hard but stay in the game. Be patient and regroup.

There is still hope for us! Don't despair in the face of failure. You can learn and change and you can still win! This is my favourite lesson of all the lessons I learnt from dominoes. This is why I am not giving up on relationships or my dream of becoming financially independent before retirement. I will stay in the game and win.

2.1 Overcoming Failure and Rejection

Finally, there are some mantras that help me to deal with failure over the years which I want to pass on.

- Perfection is the enemy of progress.
- Failing at something does not make you a failure.
- Celebrate your journey/progress not just the destination
- "Every master was once a disaster"- T. Harvey Eker
- We all wobble before we walk.

In remembering these mantras, I give myself permission to fail and get better along the way. I hope these will help you to handle failure and rejection better and give you the courage to rise above it.

Chapter 3:
REINVENTION

"Yesterday is history, tomorrow is a mystery, today is a gift of God, which is why we call it the present. Life can only be understood backwards; but it must be lived forwards. You realize that our mistrust of the future makes it hard to give up the past."

—Bill Keane

3.0
A FRESH START

The reasons for reinvention and the path to reinvention vary from one individual to another. Some persons are forced to reinvent because they were fired from the job or made redundant; for some, their company closed or a loved one died. For some, it is the pain of staying at the current level while envisioning the prospect of a brighter future. Some people have a burning desire for a dream which they just can't get rid of, and are willing to risk it all to fulfil it, even if they are financially unstable. For some, it is a pursuit of purpose or a higher call.

In my own case, I reinvented my life and career three times. In my last reinvention, I felt a pull in a new direction and felt the leading of God to do what I am now doing. I was not financially stable when I did it but I knew the God who gives the mission and the vision will also grant the provision. I established reasons to take the risks to engage in entrepreneurship and ministry at the same time.

When I began writing this book, I was in year three of my current reinvention as Authorpreneur, coach and speaker. Some days were rough but I kept my eyes on the rewards and the reasons because I was determined to make it work. At this stage of your life, do you feel the desire to reinvent your life and career? Are you merely working for survival rather than significance? Are you struggling to make ends meet while you work? Are you miserable with your current job? Is there a fresh desire to pursue your dream that has been delayed?

If so, how do you reinvent when the risks are greater? How do you reinvent or redesign your life to chase your childhood dreams when you have children who are depending on you, and you are not financially secure? While the dynamics of reinvention will be different for everyone, it starts with a belief that it is possible. The stories in Part 1 are evidence of this and once we know it is possible, we can find a way to make it happen.

Therefore, let's consider some general steps to reinvent your life particularly when your risks are greater by virtue of family responsibilities or financial insecurity. If believing it is possible is the first step, the next step is to count the cost. The following questions can help you to count the cost:

a. Why do you still need to pursue this dream or reinvent your life and career?

b. How will this improve your life or your family's life?

c. What are the benefits or rewards for doing so?

d. What is the true state of your finances?

e. How much will it cost to pursue this dream?

f. How long will it take?

g. When is the right time to do it?

h. What are the pathways to accomplish your dream?

3.0 A Fresh Start

i. Who has done this before?

j. How much information have you gathered by way of research or speaking to others who've accomplished this dream?

k. What investments or sacrifices will you have to make?

l. What lifestyle changes will be required?

m. What are the obstacles and what can you do to prevent them?

n. How can you invest in personal growth and self-development?

Reinvention is not an overnight process. It took my mother six years to matriculate to Nursing School. James Altucher, the author of the book *Reinvent Yourself,* notes that reinvention is often a 3-5-year process and depending on the dream, it may take longer. Therefore, you will have to plan carefully and exercise patience.

If the dream is a business, know that 85% of start-ups fail in the first five years. In the first two years, very often you are operating at a loss; in the next two years you may break even and then in the 5th year, if you stay the course, you may begin to see real profit.

Although not shared in the excerpt, part of what my Mom did was to ensure each of her children had a skill or some stepping stone for self-sustenance before she pursued her dream fully. She sent me to Teachers' College, my sister to Nursing School and my brother was an apprentice to auto-electrical mechanic at our church. Thus, she did not have to worry about her children when she pursued her dream.

She also made financial provision by having an emergency fund. She obtained a scholarship from her workplace to further her studies. This was the first time someone in her position (a Ward Assistant) received such a scholarship in the history of the organization. It was a miracle! You have to believe that miracles will happen along the way.

My Mom used our textbooks to study for some of her subjects on her own. The ones she could not teach herself she learnt formally. How can you invest in your own self-development? A specialist in any area is merely one who has studied the area and has greater knowledge in that field than the average person. Whatever the dream is, you can begin to study on your own. In this age of the internet and YouTube, audio books, free online learning platforms and the like, you can pretty much learn almost anything you want without setting foot in a traditional classroom. Success expert, Brian Tracy, says it takes 5-7 years to become an expert in your field. This can be obtained by studying one hour per day for 5-7 years.

10 Reinvention Tips

From my personal experience of re-invention, I want to recommend the following 10 tips to make the process a smooth one.

1. *Strategy*: Decide what you want and devise a strategy (design) to get it.

2. *Count the cost*: What resources will you need? Whose help do you need in the process? How much time and effort will be needed?

3.0 A Fresh Start

3. *Skill development*: Consider the skills you already have and what new skills you need to learn.

4. *Financial assessment*: Assess your finances and financial commitments—Do you have an emergency fund of at least US$1000 or J$100,000? Can you pay the rent or mortgage for the next three to six months without a job? If not, set up one before you jump, if at all possible.

5. *Exercise courage and patience*: Feel the fear and do it anyway but do not expect overnight success. It will be rough for a while.

6. *Establish your why:* Your reason (s) will be your rod and staff and the oxygen that keeps you breathing when the process gets challenging, and it will. Write down five to ten reasons why you need to reinvent and still chase that dream.

7. *Get support*: You cannot reinvent alone. This support could come in the form of an online community or simply one or two friends who will cheer you on. Don't go it alone. You may need to enlist others to help in the care of your children if they are still young. Sometimes you know what to do but can't seem to translate knowledge to action. In this case, get a coach, attend training events and get an accountability partner.

8. *Success models*: On your journey, you will need some inspiration. Who are the folks who have travelled this path successfully before? What lessons can you learn from them? Meditate on their stories continually. I have

found this really helps especially when the process gets challenging.

9. *Learn more to earn more*: Life-long learning is a must. You will need new skills on your reinvention journey in order to do it successfully.

10. *Seek Divine aid, guidance and assurance*: When we commit our plans to God and trust in Him, He will make them come to pass if it is His will. I have scriptures to which I run for constant inspiration. They are my reinvention life verses when things get tough. Prayer is what keeps me going. In my times of prayer, I get ideas and inspiration which help me to stay the course and achieve my goals.

Remember, every transition should be properly planned especially when children are involved. Unless fired, do not just leave your job like that. Simplify your lifestyle or see if you can find an additional job or study part-time while you work on your dream. There are many who make their transition slowly in this manner. If you are more on the adventurous side, take the jump but consider the consequences carefully. There will be obstacles, including people who think you are crazy.

There is safety and wisdom in the multitude of counsel (Proverbs 11:14). Get a mentor or different mentors and coaches if possible. Having a mentor or coach is one of the fastest ways to successfully redesign your life. I also recommend doing a self-inventory to find out your preferred career path and personality type.

There is a movement called Live Your Legend, founded by Scott Dinsmore. They have some useful tools to help people who want to do work they love. On their website are free

3.0 A Fresh Start

resources to help you as you reinvent. This includes a free readiness to change test which you can take to confirm or assess your readiness for change. Visit https://liveyourlegend.net/ for more information. Remember, count the cost and plan well. Life does not get better by chance; it gets better by design.

3.1
LIFE CHANGE BY DESIGN

In my second reinvention in 2010, I heard a presentation by author and business philosopher, Jim Rohn, which challenged me in a new direction. These were the words that changed my life:

> Here is a good question to ask yourself: Ten years from now you will surely arrive. The question is, where?... In 10 years, we'll arrive at either a well-designed destination or an un-designed destination... We don't want to kid ourselves about where; we don't want to kid ourselves about the road we're walking... Now's the time to fix the next 10 years... Here's what we don't want to engage in: disillusion —hoping without acting; wishing without doing. The key is to take a look and say, where am I? What could I do to make the changes to make sure that I can take more certain daily steps toward the treasure I want, the mental treasure, the personal treasure, the spiritual treasure, the financial treasure?

At that time, I was planning to be married for the first time and transitioning to a new life and career as a full-time missionary but something was not right. I felt frustrated and unhappy in my relationship but feared the consequences of a

3.1 Life-Change by Design

breakup, and I did not have the courage to walk away until that fateful night.

One night while feeling depressed, I was browsing through various videos on YouTube when I stumbled upon a motivational speaker by the name of Les Brown. He was addressing a very large crowd at the Georgia Dome, and I was completely captivated watching this man speak. He said words that deeply impacted me, "It's possible... It's not over until I win."

I felt tremendous hope from those words and posted them on my living room wall. As I continued to listen, Les Brown spoke about the dangers of being in a toxic relationship. He said, "Toxic relationships can ruin your life." Upon hearing this, I found the courage to end the relationship.

Soon after meeting Les Brown, I met Jim Rohn, and learnt about the power of goal setting. Rohn taught me how to practically set a better sail in life. He taught me, "**It's not the wind that blows, but it's the set of the sails.**" He also taught me the value of ensuring you get to a well-designed destination rather than an un-designed one.

My question to you is this, where do you want to be in the next 10 years? In 2014, after another broken engagement, God gave me a new design for my life and I am currently four years into it. Since 2014, I have seen phenomenal growth and my life has been transformed. There is, however, more to be done because it is still early days.

If you have faced many challenges and setbacks, it's time to set a better sail and redesign your life so that the next decade will be better and greater than the previous years. I believe that once you have a design to win (a picture of your preferred future, a purpose for that future and an action plan to bring that picture to life, along with the right attitude and measures of accountability) you can win despite the odds. This is our Design to Win process in a nutshell.

Don't be afraid to set a new sail after a "hit." I am convinced that no matter how bad it is or how bad it gets, it's still possible to win! The core message of this book is, you can still win no matter how long it takes.

> **You can still win no matter how long it takes.**

The Design to Win Pledge

In my mentoring programs, career guidance classes and speeches, I usually ask participants to repeat this pledge inspired by Les Brown's presentation titled, "It's Not Over Until You Win."

There is greatness in me
It's possible to live my dreams
No matter how bad it is or how bad it gets
I'm going to make it
With Faith, courage and consistent action
I'm going to make it
It's not over until I win!

3.2
YOUR DESIGN TO WIN FRAMEWORK

In this edition of the *Design to Win Road Map*, I will be using the PAPA framework to help you create a new plan to win as you get older. The remainder of this book will focus on this PAPA framework. See the outline of the framework below.

Past| Present| Personality Profile| Purpose| Preferred Future| Picture (s) of Hope

Action

Plan

Action| Accountability| Art of Life Hurdling| Acquisition of Skills and Resources

Our PAPA framework is informed by the original design for humankind found in Genesis 1-2 of the Bible. I believe that every Design to Win should seek to recreate as much as possible the original design for humankind's life as seen in Genesis 1-2 in the Bible. Those chapters provide the foundation of all our human pursuit. Chapter three of that book reveals what went wrong and also gives us a promise of hope for the future.

3.2 Your Design to Win Framework

In the original design for life, humankind is made to be trustees of the earth. Humankind is made on purpose with a purpose. The first humans had a clear assignment and a clear purpose. They were blessed, which means among other things, *empowered to prosper*.

The first humans were lacking in nothing; they had a home (Eden) where there was no sickness, strife, poverty, hunger, disease, depression, violence or any malady. They had a perfect relationship with their Creator and lived in complete harmony as a married couple.

As I look at our world, I realize that all we chase (family, meaning, significance, wealth, well-being etc.) were all part of the original design before the villain of humanity and the enemy of the Creator, influenced the first humans to rebel against their Creator. As a consequence of their rebellion, we are all struggling today to make sense of our world. But there is hope. The Creator made a promise that one day, an offspring of the first couple would settle the score and ensure that an Eden-like existence is recreated.

As a Christian, I believe Jesus Christ is that offspring who came to undo what the enemy of humanity did, and He invites us to join Him in recreating an Eden-like existence until He returns. This is a core part of the worldview that shapes our Design to Win Road Map.

We, therefore, must find our purpose and walk in it as part of the group of earth's custodians. We have a job to do and we will be held accountability for how we live our lives just as the first humans were held accountable.

In the same way, I went all the way back to the origin of life to create a system to win, the new design for your life must begin with an analysis of your past and an evaluation of your present life before you can plan ahead.

Examine yourself to understand your personality profile and gifting. Determine or clarify your unique purpose in life. Once you get a clear picture of your past, present and personality profile, you can begin to create a picture of your preferred future.

Gather pictures or symbols of hope to help you to persevere along the journey because that villain of humanity still exists as well as other human villains and our own internal struggles. There will be many obstacles to prevent your progress both internal and external; mentally, physically, emotionally, financially, relationally, spiritually and the like.

A picture of hope can be an image from nature, a prophetic promise, a role model etc. which motivates you to stay the course. With these pictures in mind, create an action plan to bring your preferred future to life. Find an accountability partner and take action. Ask your Creator for help each step of the way and take action.

Planning without action is futile. We must take actions to implement the plan despite the challenges. Only then can we win. To help you implement your plan, our Design to Win system of accountability includes checks at intervals of 30 or 90 days and sometimes up to one year. We also include something called the Art of Life Hurdling to teach you some key principles and techniques to overcome failure, financial challenges, low productivity and disappointments.

I have seen tremendous results with my clients who have employed our Design to Win system. I have included one testimonial below from my client Kerone Edwards, who completed a six-week Design to Win programme with me in 2019.

> I am really grateful for your motivation in this season of my life. I am more involved at work meetings. I have hit the 10

3.2 Your Design to Win Framework

million target goal even before the time... I am mentoring the young lady. We have been sharing and I am doing my best to keep her empowered... working on spending more time in the Word of God... I am more determined to live an overcoming life no matter what.

Now that you have a better understanding of the process and an idea of its impact, let's look at some activities which you can do to implement this framework.

Chapter 4
A JOURNEY OF SELF-DISCOVERY

"The best work, the best career, for you, the one that makes you happiest and most fulfilled, is going to be the one that uses: your favourite transferable skills, in your favourite subjects, fields or special knowledges, in a job that offers you your preferred people environments, your preferred working conditions, with your preferred salary or other rewards, working towards your preferred goals and values."

—Dick Bolles

4.0
GETTING A PICTURE OF YOUR PAST AND PRESENT LIFE

We begin with our True Life–Winner Test adopted from the late motivational guru, Zig Ziglar. While each person defines success (winning) in a different way, Zig Ziglar's assessment is a good tool to measure a winning life and career. Winning means doing well in the following eight areas:

1. **Career**: Doing well in a chosen field.

2. **Attitude**: Freedom from fear and worry and having a positive mental attitude.

3. **Spiritual**: Having peace with God, peace of mind.

4. **Finances**: Reasonably stable, prosperous and secure.

5. **Relationships**: Happy and healthy relationships with friends and family.

6. **Personal**: Achieving set goals.

4.0 Getting a Picture of Your Past and Present Life

7. **Health**: Physical and emotional health.

8. **Hope for the future.**

Winning should be measured holistically. It is about fulfilling your God-given purpose and using your best gifts and passion to achieve your chief life and career goals, while making a difference in the world. Winning is about standing in storms, bouncing back from adversity and maintaining your hope. It is really about restoring Eden and all that was lost in the original design.

I recommend using a scale of 1-10, with 10 being the highest, to rate yourself in each of these areas. If you score 5 and over in most of these categories, I would say you are on the winning path.

NOTE: In our system, there can be no eternal win without a relationship with God. According to Jesus of Nazareth, "It does not profit to gain the whole world and lose your soul" (Mark 8:36).

TRUE LIFE-WINNER TEST

On a scale of 1-10, with ten being the highest, how would you rate yourself in these 8 areas?

1. *Career*: doing well in a chosen field _____

2. *Attitude*: freedom from fear and worry—positive mental attitude _____

3. *Spiritual*: peace with God and peace of mind _____

Design to Win Road Map 2

4. *Finances:* reasonably stable, prosperous and secure _____

5. *Relationships*: happy and healthy relationships with friends and family _____

6. *Personal*: achieving set goals _____

7. *Health:* physical and emotional health _____

8. *Hope* (for the future) _____

4.1
THE DESIGN TO WIN SURVEY

For things to change, one has to do a rigorous life-analysis and then plan the way forward. I created the Design to Win Survey to help clients analyze their lives.

I use it to get a picture of who they are, understand their past and present and get a vision of where they would like to go. The survey responses are then used to plan for their progress.

The survey can be completed in 30-45 minutes. Complete both Sections A and B. If doing a coaching or mentoring program, submit your answers to your instructor/coach. It would be wise to set up a coaching or consultation session to discuss the results and the way forward. Answer all questions in Section A and the relevant ones in Section B.

SECTION A

1. Do you find yourself constantly dwelling on past successes or failures? [ ] Yes   [ ] No

2. Do you learn something valuable from all mistakes? [ ] Yes [ ] No

3. Does life seem futile and the future hopeless to you?
[ ] Yes [ ] No

4. Do you have a plan for your life for the next 5 years?
[ ] Yes [ ] No

4b. IF YES, Is this plan in writing? [ ] Yes [ ] No

5. Do you consider your mind a resource? [ ] Yes [ ] No

6. Do you have a habit of saving? [ ] Yes [ ] No —If yes, do you have 1-3 months' salary or expenses saved?
[ ] Yes [ ] No

7. Do you suffer from any of these fears?

- Fear of poverty [ ] Yes [ ] No
- Fear of criticism [ ] Yes [ ] No
- Fear of ill health [ ] Yes [ ] No
- Fear of loss of love of someone [ ] Yes [ ] No
- Fear of old age [ ] Yes [ ] No
- Fear of death [ ] Yes [ ] No
- Fear of failure [ ] Yes [ ] No
- Fear of rejection [ ] Yes [ ] No
- Other fears: List them

8. Do you believe you were created for a special purpose? [ ] Yes [ ] No —If yes, what is that purpose?

9. Do you believe in life after death? [ ] Yes [ ] No
Explain your answer.

4.1 The Design to Win Survey

10. Do you know or have ideas about the contribution you would like to make to society before you die?
    [ ] Yes   [ ] No —If yes, describe briefly or list them.

11. Name 3 of your strengths or things that you are really good at.

12. Name 3 of your most damaging weaknesses and what you are doing to correct them.

13. Reflect on and review the last 10 years of your life. As you review and answer the questions below, bear in mind the following areas to guide your answers: material and financial; spiritual, mental and emotional; career and education; relationships; health and recreation; and service and contribution.

    a. What have you accomplished in the last 10 years of your life that you are proud of or consider to be significant? List 5-10 things.

    b. What do you wish you had accomplished? List 1-3 things.

    c. Why didn't you accomplish them? List 1-3 reasons.

14. If enough money was not an obstacle, describe what your ideal life and career/work would look like? For example: Where would you go? What would you like to have, own, see or do? List as many things as possible.

15. List 1-3 things which you feel are or have been obstacles to your progress. These include significant habits, attitudes, heartaches and patterns which have been holding you back.

16. How would you describe your relationship with these persons? Use the terms satisfactory, excellent, poor, undecided, non-existent, not applicable to describe each:
    a. Your father (deceased or alive)
    b. Your Mother (deceased or alive)
    c. Friends (Past and present)
    d. Siblings and other relatives
    e. Schoolmates
    f. Work colleagues
    g. Spouse/partner
    h. Children

17. Who among your acquaintances, associates, friends or family:

    - Encourages you the most?
    - Cautions you the most?
    - Discourages you the most?

18. How much of your time out of every 24 hours do you devote to:

    - Occupation/school work _____
    - Sleep _____
    - Play/relaxation/socializing _____
    - Acquiring useful knowledge _____
    - Plain waste _____

19. What do you think about the idea of becoming rich?

20. What connection, if any, do you see between the people with whom you associate most closely and any unhappiness you have been experiencing?

SECTION B
REINVENTION QUESTIONS

1. If you had to live your life all over again, what are the things you would not get into again? Think of your work, family, friends, community, spiritual life, etc. and list 5 -10 things.

2. If you could not do your present job anymore, but you received 10 million US dollars and never had to work again, what would you spend your time volunteering to do?

3. What are the fields that you most enjoy exploring in magazines, books, seminars, workshop, the internet and life in general?

4. What experiences have you had thus far in life that made you excited in which you felt you did well? List or describe 3-5 of these.

5. If you had to visit different work settings in order to learn more about them, which ones would you most likely visit? List 3-5.

6. How could you plan to have more leisure time or more time with loved ones and friends in the present rather than waiting for retirement?

7. What would be your preferred monthly salary range from lowest to highest?

4.2
YOUR PERSONALITY AND CAREER PROFILE

These instruments can help you to choose or change careers and assess your options. They are also used in job interviews and in assigning persons to work in different teams. I have provided the links to these free tools, which you can use to discover your personality type and career possibilities.

Visit the links provided to do the Kiersey Temperament Sorter Test, Holland's Code Career Test and the Strength Finder Test. An alternative to the Holland's code is Richard Bolles's Party Exercise which can be done in less than 5 minutes. If you do have a copy of What Colour is Your Parachute? (2018), it's included on pages 132-133.

You can also simply Google all these tests: Holland's Code Career Test, The Party Exercise/ Holland Party Game, Kiersey Temperament Test and The Strength Finder Aptitude Test.

- Holland's Career Code Test, https://www.truity-.com/test/holland-code-career-test/

- Kiersey Temperament Sorter, https://www.keirsey.com/sorter/register.aspx

- Strength Finder Aptitude Test, http://www.richard-step.com/-richard-step-strengths-weaknesses-aptitude-test/free-aptitude-test-find-your-strengths-weaknesses-online-version/

Type in your 3-letter Holland code using O*NET or visit Holland's Code Occupation Database–VISTa Life/Career Cards to get more information concerning your career/occupational interests (http://www.vista-cards.com/occupations/).

Then click on the occupations of interest to see what tasks, skills, knowledge, abilities, work context and education are required for those occupations.

Upon completion of these tests, answer the following questions:

a) Identify your personality type and record a brief description of the same.

b) Note three of your strengths and weaknesses.

c) Identify at least 10 career or occupational options or interests.

Chapter 5
UNDERSTANDING PURPOSE

The accomplishment of purpose is better than profit.
—African Proverb

5.0
WHAT IS YOUR PURPOSE IN LIFE?

The late Caribbean leadership expert and author extraordinaire, Dr. Myles Munroe posits, "The greatest tragedy in life is not death but a life lived without purpose." The first major decision we should make in designing our preferred future is to determine our unique purpose in life. Author Napoleon Hill reminds us, "all successful persons have a chief definite aim in life." Success is the accomplishment of our divine purpose and doing it effectively.

According to Munroe, "Purpose is when you know and understand what you were born to accomplish." Your Great Designer (God) had a purpose in mind for you when He created you. That purpose is your reason to travel on planet Earth. Failure to understand your purpose will prevent you from getting to your destination in life and being left at the bottom of the pile.

North America's most renowned leadership expert, Dr. John Maxwell, has said in several of his presentations that the two most important days of your life are, "the day when you were born and the day you discover why." What profound statements on purpose!

5.0 What is Your Purpose in Life?

When you discover why you were born, it is then that you really start living with purpose. Knowing your purpose will benefit you in at least seven ways. You will:

a. Become successful or achieve more in life.

b. Use your time better.

c. Focus better and give attention to things that really matter.

d. Follow your dreams instead of the dreams of others.

e. Gain courage and strength in the face of problems.

f. Have a reason to live.

g. Improve your decision-making.

General Purpose vs. Unique Purpose

According to world renowned career coach and former Episcopalian minister, Dr. Richard Bolles, our purpose is our chief mission in life, and this inevitably lands us in the "lap of God." This God-factor is often missing from conversations on purpose in the Western Hemisphere where a belief in God is seen as foolish. Bolles gives us three levels of purpose which I have reframed as follows:

1. *Recognizing God's Presence* (Shared Purpose): A core part of humankind's purpose is to be ever conscious of God's presence, hour by hour and living to please God.

2. *Making the World a Better Place* (Shared): Part of humankind's purpose is: "to do what you can, moment by moment, day by day, step by step to make this world a better place, following the leading and guidance of God's Spirit within and around you."

3. *Making a Difference with Your Greatest Gifts and Talents* (Unique): Your unique purpose is "to exercise the Talent that you particularly came to earth to use that is, your greatest gift, which you delight to use, in the place(s) or setting (s) that God has caused to appeal to you the most, and for the purposes that God most needs to have done in the world" (2018, 280).

6 Ways to Discover Your Unique Purpose

1. *Pain and Solutions*: It is in finding solutions to the problems around us or things that cause us or someone else pain that some of us find our purpose. That which causes us pain is sometimes the flipside of our purpose. By this, I mean that the very things which cause us pain are the very problems we are called or created to solve. When we find solutions to these struggles, we can then help others who are now struggling with the issues we have conquered and thus serve a unique purpose in the world. This is bringing comfort to others with the comfort we ourselves have received (2 Corinthians 1:4).

2. *Gifts and Passion*: We accomplish our unique purpose by using our gifts, passions, talents, training and resources to solve a problem for a particular

5.0 What is Your Purpose in Life?

group (s) of people for the glory of God. It is about making a difference in the lives of people. We can recognize our individual unique purpose (doing what we were made to do), when we find ourselves loving what we do.

3. *Being Lost in Service*: We can recognize our unique purpose when we are engaged in an activity that causes us to lose all sense of time, or an activity that creates a deep level of satisfaction. I know when I am walking in purpose. I lose track of time doing it and I come alive doing it.

4. *Divine Revelation*: This is a supernatural revelation and famous biblical examples include John the Baptist, Jesus of Nazareth, Sampson, Abraham and the Apostle Paul. In the case of Jesus, John and Sampson, an angel appeared to their parents to convey the purpose of the child. Abraham had an encounter with God when his purpose was revealed.

    Sometimes it is a vision or dream or just a strong impression in your heart or God may send someone to tell you. This was the case with the Apostle Paul when Ananias came to him and told him what God was calling him to do. In my case, God revealed to three ministers what he wanted me to do and when they told me, it resonated with me and gave me a reason to live when I wanted to die.

5. *Reflection/Introspection/Self-Questioning*: This is pretty much asking yourself strategic questions about your passion, gifts, experiences, major concerns and the difference you would like to make

in the world. It includes reflecting on your life and what matters most to you or where you were happiest or saddest and making a decision to do something about it.

6. *Feedback from Others*: Sometimes others will see in you what you cannot see in yourself. This is about getting suggestions from individuals about what you are really good at, and persons pointing out the attributes and natural tendencies they observe about you. You can also use feedback to confirm the desires in your heart. Make note of what others say and be willing to try it.

NOTE: It usually takes a while to understand your purpose. It can take years for some people to recognize their unique purpose. Reflect on the methods outlined above and pray for God to reveal to you His purpose for your life. In addition to this, note the following:

1. *It is not about you:* Your unique individual purpose is connected with helping and serving others. It is making a contribution to others using your unique gifts/skills to make a difference in the lives of the people to whom you are drawn.

2. *Gifts are the means*: How you serve and define your contribution will be based on your gifts, passion, beliefs/values and the problems or pain that matter most to you that you.

3. *Different expressions*: Your purpose statements may change over time and that's okay. What matters is

5.0 What is Your Purpose in Life?

finding a compelling why for living and acting in accordance with it, so that you do not merely exist or drift aimlessly in life.

5.1
PURPOSE-DISCOVERY ACTIVITIES

Option A

Find a nice quiet place, grab a sheet of paper and use this pool of 21 questions to guide you in discovering your purpose. One of the blockages to recognizing purpose is technology and busyness. You have to block out distractions to hear your heart or God's voice so you can recognize your purpose.

Answer as many questions as you feel are necessary. Examine your answers. Are big concepts emerging? Are there recurring ideas or things? Note these! These are big clues if not answers to your purpose. Summarize your answers to create a statement of purpose.

20 Purpose Discovery Questions

If you are a person of faith, make sure you pray for a revelation regarding your purpose as you seek to answer these questions.

1. What is my chief definite aim in life?

2. What are the uses of my life?

5.1 Purpose Discovery Activities

3. What talents and gifts do I have?

4. How could my talents and gifts be used to serve others in an amazing way?

5. What burning problems do I feel called to solve or fix?

6. What irritates me or makes me sad?

7. What life issue causes me the greatest pain?

8. What makes me happy or causes me to smile?

9. What is it that I see in life that I feel I could improve or change?

10. What difference do I wish to make in the world?

11. What ideas do I have that will not go away?

12. What legacy do I want to leave for my family or country?

13. What is the most important goal that I want to achieve in life?

14. What mark do I want to leave in this world after I die?

15. What does God want me to do with my life?

16. What is the greatest service I feel I could make to mankind?

17. What is it that when I do it, I feel most alive, satisfied, confident or fulfilled?

18. What work would I love to do even if I were not paid for it?

19. What one thing do I want to be known for when others call my name?

20. With what do others most identify me?

Option B

Think of your greatest struggles, pains and concerns, along with your gifts and abilities. Identify the people who share your struggles. Who are they and how will you help them with the gifts, passions, training and skills you possess? What do you feel God is calling you to do?

Use one of the structures and examples below as a guide to write your purpose statement or create something original.

For example, I help (verb) authors in the Caribbean (target/audience and place) to transform lives and create sustainable income with non-fiction books (activity and solution).

I_____(verb) _____(target group or kind of people) in _____(place in the world) to _____ (activity/difference/solution to problem).

OR

5.1 Purpose Discovery Activities

To raise up author-transformers from the Caribbean and the Diaspora to transform lives and change the perception and economy of our region.

To_____(verb/phrase) _____ (target group and place in the world) to _____ (activity, difference or solution to problem).

Other Purpose Statement Examples and Taglines

- To empower people around the world through education, writing and speaking.

- To serve as a leader, live a balanced life, and apply godly principles to make a significant difference.

- To use my sporting talent to help people

- To use my influence and gifts to build a home to care for orphans.

- To be a teacher and to be known for inspiring my students to be more than they thought they could be.

- To use my gifts of intelligence, charm and optimism to build the self-worth of women around the world.

- To inspire people to live healthier lives. Tagline: inspiration and health.

- To exalt God and empower people to win at life. Tagline: Exalt God... Empower People.

- To help people to win at work and succeed at life. Tagline: Win at work... succeed at life.

- To help people to live vibrant lives. Tagline: Vibrant Living.

- To inspire people through art. Tagline: Art is life.

- CMC – Cover, Mobilize and Connect people in missions

- RUTH –Raise Up the Hurting/ Helpless/Hopeless

5.2
ENVISIONING YOUR PREFERRED FUTURE

According to Dr. Richard Bolles, "The world is astonished when it meets someone who knows where they are going with their life; that is such a rare kind of strength." It's time to figure out where you are going with your life. Now that you have a better understanding of your past, present, personality type, gifting, career options and your purpose, let's create a vision of your preferred future.

According to Stephen Covey, author of *The 7 Habits of Highly Effective People*, "start with the end in mind." All designers, including the Creator start with the end in mind and then work backwards to make it happen. For example, an architect designs a house before building; a travel agent choosing the destination before planning the route to get there.

What is your vision of your ideal destination in life? What does a winning life and career look like for you? Your 1-5-year progress plan must be a subset of this larger life-vision. Your accomplishments in these years must be stops along the way to eventually get to that ultimate destination.

Thinking and acting this way will ensure you live a purpose-driven life. It is also the way to "astonish the world" because you will be living with a sense of direction; knowing where you want to go and what you want to do with your life. Let's picture the entire house, create a blueprint to build it and build it block upon block until it is finished.

Note: Our definition of a true life-winner is one who thinks of earthly and eternal destination points. Include both in your vision.

Always pen your vision. Successful people think long term and think on paper. They set goals, make plans and put their plans in writing. They "pen it to win." No architect or designer keeps the sketch in his head. The architect always has a blueprint. Imagine what would happen if you tried to construct a building without one! In many countries like Jamaica, it is illegal to build without a plan or blueprint approved by the parish council or relevant authority.

Pen it, to not forget it. Pen it, to communicate it. Pen it, so what's in your mind's eye can be brought to light. Pen it, to gather resources. Pen it, for greater insights and aid. Pen it, to seize opportunities. Pen it, lest you give up or forget when there are lengthy delays, detours and disappointments. Pen it, so that the vision will live and not die. Pen it, for your personal accountability.

ACTIVITY

Choose one of the three options provided to decide your ideal life and career destination. When you choose your option, write it in the past tense, because the idea is capturing the end, which means you already did these things.

You can make a list or write a nice paragraph or two. Use a eulogy, citation or tribute to you at age 80. You may find sample tributes, obituaries or short citations to guide you in

5.2 Envisioning Your Preferred Future

preparing to write yours. These can be found online or via a local newspaper.

Use these guiding questions to help you create this vision. You do not need to answer them individually.

a. What was your greatest contribution or legacy to community, country or family?

b. What educational or career pursuits did you follow?

c. Did you work or start your own business?

d. Did you write anything?

e. What were you like with friends and family?

f. How many children or grandchildren did you have?

g. What did people appreciate most about you?

h. What organizations or groups were you part of?

i. What about your principles and personality?

Option 1: The End of Your Life—Eulogy / Obituary / Death Tribute

Fast forward to the end of your life, imagine it's your funeral or an article is written about you in the newspaper upon your death. What is it that you would want them to say about you, in no more than 250 words? In your description, be as concise and specific as possible about the things that would really matter to you or you would really want to be remembered for above everything else.

Option 2: A Living Tribute at 80 years old

Fast forward to age 80. There is a function being held in your honour, perhaps a birthday party or some honorary function put on by family or colleagues. What would they say about you? Your description should be as concise as possible about the things that would really matter to you. What 3-10 things would really want to be remembered for above everything else?

Option 3: Your Legacy—Citation

Fast forward to age 80 and on a special occasion, you are presented with a citation, no more than 250 words. What would be the content of your citation? Be as concise and specific as possible about the 3-10 things that really mattered to you and what you accomplished. Describe your defining legacy.

CHAPTER 6:
CREATING YOUR ACTION PLAN

Tomorrow belongs to the people who prepare for it today.
—African Proverb

6.0
SETTING MAJOR LIFE GOALS

Now that you have chosen your ultimate destination in life or your preferred future, let's identify some stops along the way, as you journey towards your preferred future. These stops are what we will refer to as short-term or long-term goals.

We will also look at some reasons and rewards for making these stops. This interim journey is estimated to be 1-5 years. You will be making key life, career and legacy decisions for your future.

Travel Smart Advisory

When it comes to setting and keeping goals, many persons struggle in this area and are sometimes dismissive. I believe we are all already goal-setters and goal-achievers, but some goals are harder to achieve than others.

If you ever travelled from one place to another or kept an appointment, that's proof you are already a goal achiever. You made a decision and acted on it. That was a goal accomplished.

6.0 Setting Major Life Goals

I believe part of the failure to keep big goals is because we do not set goals in writing with definite plans to achieve them. Sometimes the timelines do not match the magnitude of the goals and at times we are discouraged.

I often cite an old Harvard Study reported by Mark McCormack in *What They Don't Teach You in the Harvard Business School* (1986) to prove the effectiveness of penning our goals with plans to accomplish them. There have also been similar studies and findings in recent times.

In 1979, interviewers asked new graduates from the Harvard MBA Program about their goals and found that:

1. 84% had no specific goals at all;
2. 13% had goals but they were not committed to paper;
3. 3% had clear, written goals and plans to accomplish them.

In 1989, the interviewers again interviewed the graduates of that class. Here are the results 10 years later:

- The 13% of the class who had goals were earning, on average, twice as much as the 84% who had no goals at all.

- Even more staggering —the 3% who had clear, written goals were earning, on average, ten times as much as the other 97% put together.

In this phase, you will be creating holistic goals in the following seven (7) areas of your life for the next 1-5 years:

a. Spiritual Development

b. Financial & Material

c. Career and Business

d. Relationships [Family and Friends]

e. Personal Growth/Self-Improvement and Learning

f. Health and Fitness

g. Social and Community Contribution

ACTION PLAN ACTIVITIES

Step 1: Preparation

- Block a time period of at least 30 minutes.
- A notepad/sheets of paper/your computer/Ipad etc. and a quiet place
- Pray and dream about the next 1-5 years.
- Remember your ultimate destination

Step 2: Select your goals

What needs to happen for you to look back and say "these were my best years?"

If money were no problem and you could live your ideal life and career, what would you want to be, do, have, achieve, etc. in the 7 areas of our true life-winner test in the next 1-5 years?

6.0 Setting Major Life Goals

We use the quick-list 30-second exercise created by success expert Brian Tracy in his book *Reinvention*. According to Tracy, "when you have only 30 seconds to write down the answers to these questions, your answers will be as accurate as if you had 30 minutes or three hours" (2009, 51-53).

Choose big goals and little goals. They could be related to simple things like vacation, birthday treats, immediate needs and major things like degrees and certifications.

As quickly as you can, in 30 seconds or less for each question, write down your answers to the following:

a. What are your three most important business and career goals right now?

b. What are your three most important family and relationship goals right now?

c. What are your three most important health and fitness goals right now?

d. What are your three most important financial goals right now?

e. What are your three most important educational or learning goals right now?

f. What are your three most important social service and community goals right now?

g. What are your three most important goals for spiritual development and inner peace right now?

Step 3: Prioritize to Optimize

According to the Pareto principle by Italian economist Vilfredo Pareto, 80% of our results come from 20% input. Your aim in this section is to identify your 20% goals that will give you 80% results. This means you need to find the one stone that can kill two or more birds. In order to do this, you must narrow down your list of goals.

Look back at your list of goals for each category and narrow down this list in each category. Put a special marker to highlight these goals. This means from a list of 21 goals that you will end up with 7 goals.

It's time to narrow down these goals even further, because if we chase too many rabbits, we will not catch any.

Imagine in 24 hours you could be granted 5 of these goals; which five would you choose? Highlight these goals.

These are the 5 most important goals that you should pursue over the next 1-5 years.

These are the goals which you will use to create your life-winning plan. In the actual doing phase of our Design to Win Road Map, you will create a list of sub-goals or steps to accomplish these goals each month and each quarter of the year.

Step 4: Personalizing your goals

Rewrite each of these goals in the present tense using "I" statements. I want to you think like a designer and write your goals as finished in your mind.

This is a form of expression of faith, seeing the end in mind—the achievement of your goals.

Be specific about those goals. Ask yourself: how much and by when? Your goals must also have a time frame and should include a verb.

6.0 Setting Major Life Goals

Use the popular acronym S.M.A.R.T. Be Specific, Measurable, Action-Oriented and Time-bound (SMART). These goals must energize you.

Your goals need to be big but not unrealistic given the timeframe you are working with (1-5 years). They also need to reflect your season of life and what you truly will commit to do.

For example:

- I save US$1000 by December 2020 —instead of "I want more money."

- I am a lawyer by December 2023 —instead of "I want to be a lawyer."

- I read one book each month—instead of "I read more."

Step 5: Reasons and Rewards

Be flexible with your timelines. Founder of Amazon, Jeff Bezos says, "We must be firm on the vision but flexible with the strategies." Every goal will be tested. Make a list of 5-10 reasons/rewards for achieving these goals no matter what. These reasons for example could be:

a. To better my family life

b. To never be hungry again/financial freedom

c. To make my mother proud

d. To leave a legacy

e. To fulfil my purpose and succeed in life

Step 6: Summarizing Your Decisions

Use the Macro Design to Win Blueprint in chapter 6.1 to capture your major decisions in the previous three phases and this one. This will become your 1-page Macro Design to Win plan. You can place your 1-page plan on a wall or in a notebook where you can revisit it daily or weekly and track your progress over time.

6.1
YOUR MACRO DESIGN TO WIN BLUEPRINT

Year: 20_____ - 20_____

My Life Purpose Statement:

My Preferred Future

My 5-7 Major Life Goals

5 Reasons/ Rewards/Benefits for Accomplishing These Goals

ACTIVITY B

Finalizing Your Action Plan

We do not only want you to set goals but to accomplish them. This requires further actions. These are as follows:

a. Review your major life goals and ensure each goal is measurable.

b. Determine the obstacles and difficulties you will have to overcome to achieve these five (5) major goals.

c. Determine the knowledge and skills that you will need to accomplish these five (5) major goals.

d. Determine the people, groups, sources of finance and organizations whose cooperation you will require to achieve these five (5) major goals.

e. Make a list of all of your answers and organize them by sequence and priority.

f. Include at least three (3) pictures in your plan to represent your future.

g. Read the 10 tips to actualize your plans.

h. Determine your chief goal from all your top seven (7), break it down using the Major Goal Breakdown Template.

i. List three (3) actions you will take immediately over the next 10 days to begin to accomplish this goal.

6.1 Your Macro Design to Win Blueprint

MAJOR GOAL BREAKDOWN TEMPLATE

Take your major goals and break them down into smaller targets. Work out a plan to achieve them. See sample below and you could also create a table instead of listing them as they are now.

5- Year Goal: I travel to 10 countries by 2024

1-Year Target: I travel to Canada and USA by December 2020

90-Day Target: I get my US Visa by December 2019

30-Day Target: I gather the funds for the visa by October 2019

Weekly Target: I save US$50 weekly towards my air-fare

Steps to Accomplish Targets: List everything you can think of.

Resources Needed: Be specific about how much money, the materials or the people/organization whose help you need. List them all out. Eg. US$2000 airfare, application forms completed, contact courier, do research, talk with mom and dad, clothes to travel, US$2000 spending money; job, automatic savings withdrawal, join a partner plan, letter of invitation etc.

Possible Obstacles: List 1-3

- May not get visa
- Raising the money
- Getting time off

Solutions to Overcome Obstacles: List 1-3

- Reapply as quickly as possible
- Get a loan, get extra job
- Check dates for leave and apply from early

Reasons/Rewards for Accomplishing Your Major Life Goals

- I have to make my children proud.

- I don't like to work for people, so that will push me harder to become an entrepreneur.

- So that I can help others.

- So that I can make my dreams come true.

- So I can make the world a better place.

6.2
TIPS TO IMPLEMENT YOUR DESIGN

Life, like travelling, comes with its share of eventualities. This means we must be flexible with our plans and our timelines. Be patient, as often there are flight delays, detours and stormy weather which may hinder travel. Use these ten tips to ensure you bring your plan to life.

1. *Act to Win.* You must take action on your plan. The farmer who does not plant cannot expect a harvest. As Nike says, "just do it!"

2. *Keep Your Goals in Sight.* Jim Rohn reminds us that "everything by longevity goes off track." Life is filled with many distractions, and things will happen that will cause us to forget what is important to us. In this regard, you can do any of the following to keep the goals in sight and alive:

    a. Create a vision board of the pictures and put it in a place that you can see it every day.

> b. Use your phone to record a congratulatory note to yourself about reaching these goals in five years. Play this note daily.
>
> c. Create a cue card of your goals and rewards and keep in your pocket, purse/wallet and look at it once or twice each day.
>
> d. Daily rewrite these goals from memory and pray over them.

3. *Discipline Your Disappointments*: Along the way, there will be disappointments. Perhaps your goals or plan will take longer to materialize than you initially thought. If so, simply reset the timelines and learn the lessons along the way. Don't give up. Learn how to handle rejection and how to overcome obstacles.

4. *Get an Accountability Partner*. This will help to keep you on track.

5. *Success Models*. Learn from the masters. Listen to their stories, read their books. This will keep you inspired on the journey. Don't be a copycat. Observe the principles and put your own spin on it. Get a mentor or coach.

6. *Network and Collaborate with Others*. You may not have the resources but learn to become resourceful. Find out how to access resources. No one succeeds alone. No architect builds alone. Form a mastermind group if necessary. Join an online group. Join associations of those in your field.

6.2 Tips to Implement Your Design to Win

7. *Practise Self-Discipline.* This is the master key to success. It is the power to make yourself do what you ought to do, whether you feel like it or not. Take consistent action.

8. *Invest Continually in Your Personal Growth.* You may need to learn some new skills to implement your design. Read continually. Listen to audio books, attend seminars and continually work on your self-development, so you can lead the field and be compensated richly. As Jim Rohn said, "success is what you attract by the person you become." When you invest in your personal growth, you are making yourself attractive and fit for use. Read or listen to audio books and podcasts in your area of interest at least one hour per day, five days each week. This will set you apart and help you lead the field.

9. *Develop Success Habits.* We are what we repeatedly do. John Maxwell talks about the law of five. Everyday do five things that will lead to your success. Success habits include reading, managing your time properly, exercising, expressing gratitude and so much more. What's key is to develop a routine that will lead to your success. Find out the habits of successful people and make them part of your life.

10. *Persevere and Maintain a Positive Attitude.* If you quit, you will never win. There will be disappointments along the journey but keep going. It's not over until you win!

Chapter 7:
THE ART OF LIFE HURDLING

"Adversity is the mother of progress."
—Mahatma Ghandi

7.0
BECOMING A LIFE-HURDLING CHAMPION

In 1996, Deon Hemmings broke the Olympic record for the 400 metres hurdles and created history by becoming the first Jamaican female Olympic champion for this event. She also became the first Jamaican woman to win a gold medal at the Olympics. Hemmings won gold in a very difficult race. This was a phenomenal achievement.

Hurdling is a difficult race. It is not so much about running but about a technique to cross over obstacles to get to the finish line. Athletes can be disqualified in these races if the technique is not properly followed. In the same way, your success in life is very much dependent on learning the techniques or strategies to overcome the hurdles or obstacles that life will throw at us. This reminds me of a quote by author Charles R. Swindoll: "LIFE IS 10% what happens to you and 90% how you react to it."

Successful life-hurdling is about learning to set a better sail. It is being determined to win gold in life, no matter what happens. It is learning to handle disappointments, misfortune, setbacks, failures, losses and other forms of adversity like a champion. It is turning tragedies into triumph and enduring.

Endurance, as theologian William Barclay notes is, "not just the ability to bear a hard thing, but to turn it into glory."

We know that in the past we took actions and experienced disappointments. Our goals were not accomplished in the timeframe we expected. But this is a new day! This time around, we will intentionally learn the skill of life-hurdling so that no matter how bad it gets, we will win or die trying.

The Recap Life-Hurdling Technique

There is a simple technique which I have used in as little as 5 minutes to overcome big or small disappointments and day-to-day obstacles. I also use it as a counselling and coaching tool when others come to me with their life challenges.

The ReCAP acronym describes a 7-step process to create a mind-shift which eventually causes a change in our emotions and behaviour. It produces insights that relieve anxiety and bring emotional healing. Very often when we are stressed, we are thinking negative thoughts which are untrue. Insight helps to expose those thoughts and brings the truth that leads to liberation. Let's now practice the ReCAP technique.

Think of a recent challenge—a disappointment, setback, heartbreak, an incident, sad news or bad report that robbed you of your joy. This could be at home, work, school, church or relational.

1. **R**ecount the incident briefly. What happened?

2. **C**apture your thoughts and feelings about the incident. Write statements or list these on a sheet of paper. If talking to someone, you can vocalize your thoughts and feelings.

3. **A**nalyze each of those thoughts and feelings for truth. Replace them or the dominant negative thought or feeling (often this is a lie) with a truth statement or a positive statement.

4. **A**ffirm yourself out loud with statements that are true or positive.

5. **P**rocess for Profit. List 1-3 ways to profit from this hurdle by considering one or all of the questions below:

    - Is there anything to be grateful for in this situation?

    - Is there any benefit/good that can come from this situation?

    - How could this lead to profit whether financial, societal or for your own development?

    - Is there any lesson that can be learnt from this situation?

    - Is there any opportunity that this experience can bring you to do something good?

7.0 Becoming a Life-Hurdling Champion

6. **P**rogress Planning: Consider the possibilities for profit, and create a strategy to profit from this situation. What will you do to make progress? How will you move forward? Write at least one action you will take or steps for progress.

7. **P**ray about the situation—your thoughts, feelings and plans.

7.1
TIME MANAGEMENT AND PRODUCTIVITY HACKS

"The key is in not spending time, but in investing it."
—Stephen R. Covey

How do you build a business and work part-time? How do you work and study at the same time? In our busy world, how do you manage a full-time job, family and social responsibilities without stressing out yourself, and yet remain productive, healthy and happy? These seven hacks are proven ways that have helped me and many others to hurdle these challenges quite well.

When you become an excellent time manager, you will feel good about yourself because you will feel you have "control" over your time. A major cause of stress is a sense of not having control over your time. When you take on new responsibilities, you have to adjust your routine. Some of us don't adjust well to new responsibilities. These hacks will help to remedy this situation.

1. Advanced Planning with Must Dos

2. Eliminate Online Distraction

3. Create 1 hour of Undisturbed Time for Work Daily

4. Track Your Time and Apprehend the Time-Wasting Culprits

5. Outsource and Delegate

6. Learn to Say "No"

7. Make Times of Rest a Priority

Advance Planning with Must Dos

According to time management expert Brian Tracy, "every minute spent in planning saves 10 minutes in execution." He encourages persons to always plan before they act. Success expert Jim Rohn says, "You must see your day before it begins. See your week before it begins." I refer to this as, "Designing the day to seize the day."

My advance planning technique includes making a list of all my tasks to be done for the week (sometimes the next 100 days) and a list of my Must Do Tasks for each day or week. To manage your time well, you must recognize that there is not enough time to do everything you want to do, but there is sufficient time to do what is most important to you. In following Tracy's expert advice, ask yourself the following questions:

- *What have I been hired to do?*
- *What is the most valuable use of my time?*
- *What results matter?*
- *What am I trying to accomplish each day and why?*
- *Which 20% of my activities will give me 80% results?*

After figuring these out, create a schedule of 5-6 key activities to be done each day and check mark your must dos for each day. Tracy in his book, *Eat That Frog*, encourages us to do our most important task first. This task very often is not pleasant and is akin to eating a frog.

In my case, I don't always do my most important/difficult task first. However, I am careful to make sure as much as possible that my must dos are done daily or weekly, and I usually get them done. Time management requires discipline and determination. Tracy notes that it's best to start off with the most important task for that day before attempting any other, because if you cannot finish everything on that list, at least getting that one out the way will make you feel accomplished.

Additionally, planning in advance eases my stress and helps me to sleep better. I don't have to wonder what to do the next day. It can also be done at the end of each work day, just before going to bed or within the first hour of the day, before you start daily activities. Now, try this hack and let me know if it works for you. Email ruthtaylor@extramileja.com.

Eliminate Online Distraction

Social media is a major time waster these days. If you do not work online and can avoid checking your email or going on

Facebook before leaving for work or school, and before accomplishing your top must do activity, you will be more productive. All of us know when we begin checking emails and Facebook, 15 minutes quickly turns into two hours. If I want to reach work on time, it is best not to go on social media early in the morning.

Here are some suggestions to eliminate or decrease the distractions: turn off your notifications, set specific times to check emails and messages, perhaps 2-3 times a day and turn off your WIFI for set periods. Exception to these guidelines may be if your work directly involves social media or you work online. I know this is extremely hard, but if we are to focus and be productive, we cannot allow the gadgets to rule us. We must master the gadgets.

Create 1 Hour of Undisturbed Time for Work Daily

The reality is many persons do not do productive work during the scheduled working hours on the job each day. Many employees waste time doing things unrelated to their jobs such as checking social media pages, engaging in idle talk or gossip and taking extended lunch breaks.

Those who operate in an office environment also know that unplanned meetings or unscheduled walk-ins often hinder our daily productivity. As success expert Brian Tracy recommends, create one (1) hour of undisturbed time to work on your major tasks. This, he explains will amount to three (3) full days of regular work. So how do we achieve this? Here are some suggestions:

7.2 Being Money Smart

1. Arrive at work earlier or work later except when working by hourly wage requiring "clock-in/out" or submitted time sheet that affects payroll.

2. If you have an office, where permitted put up a "no disturb" or "meeting in progress" sign.

3. Turn off your WIFI or put your phone on silent.

4. Ask your secretary or relevant person to hold all calls for an hour except for emergencies.

5. Let persons know your undisturbed times, so they do not interrupt except for a work-related emergency.

6. Start your day earlier before everyone else rises and get the work done before you leave home.

Finally, notes Tracy, when you are at work, "work all the time you work." When you don't work all the time you are at work, you have to take work home. This encroaches on your family time and robs them of your valuable presence.

Track Your Time and Apprehend the Time-Wasting Culprits

According to Tracy, "time management is life management." In order to be an effective time manager, you must desire it, decide to act, be disciplined and determined, or it will not work. One of the ways to increase and improve your time management is by tracking your time and apprehending time-wasting culprits.

If time is money, then we need to know how we spend it. What if you had a business and never knew where the money went month after month and week after week? I'm sure that would be a recipe for disaster, so why are we so casual about our time? No wonder we are stressed! If you don't know concretely how you are spending your time, there is no way you can concretely determine how to save, trim or redirect energies and activities.

Tracking is a good way to assess any area of your life that is causing stress. Just the notion of observation makes you more careful in your actions. In 2015, I tracked my time for the week and noted my activities for each hour and then at the end of the week; I did an assessment. I knew I spent a lot of time on the internet, but I was shocked by the number of hours, and it was not all on productive activities. I realized that even though I need to work online, I could make that time more efficient by scheduling set times for research or socializing.

Tracking works! I did the same thing with my finances and tracked my expenditures over the course of 31 days. Once again, I was shocked at how much I was spending on transportation. Since then, I have been able to reduce my travel costs by 60%.

If you want to get control of your time, you've got to know concretely where it all goes. Only then can you apprehend the time-wasting culprits and begin to take corrective measures. I would recommend tracking at the end of every quarter to measure your progress. Try it and let me know your results.

Outsource and Delegate

Have you read *The 4-Hour Work Week* by Timothy Ferris? This is a fantastic book, if you desire to be more productive. Two of the concepts it discusses are "outsourcing" and "delegating." According to productivity specialist Michael Hyatt, you should delegate something, if you find someone who can do it 70% as well as you.

7.2 Being Money Smart

Many persons struggle with delegation because of perfectionist tendencies, trust issues and concerns about quality. If you expand your services and intend to be very successful, you will need to delegate. You cannot succeed alone. Yes, it will take time to teach before you delegate, but in the end, it will save you time.

Outsourcing is similar. It is directing/sending the task to someone else who is more competent and skilled than you are or simply because you prefer not to be saddled with it. You can outsource sub-tasks to free up time to work on your main task.

For example, Amazon is a great outsourcing platform which sells and distributes my books all over the world. This saves me from the stress of delivery and shipping. Fiverr is another great outsourcing site, where you can find qualified persons to do various tasks at an affordable rate. I use them to outsource some of my book publishing process, and it makes my life easier.

When outsourcing and delegating, act with clarity. Be very, very clear on what you want, and describe this in great detail, so that the person or company can follow your instructions well. Having a virtual assistant is another means of outsourcing or delegating. We can hire virtual assistants to get some administrative tasks done at a fairly cheap rate.

These virtual assistants can be in different time zones. In this way, while we sleep, someone is working on a task important to us, which will be ready when we start our work day in our own time zone. The things you do not like to do, that are not in line with your expertise should be outsourced or delegated.

I generally outsource parts of my projects, and this both reduces my stress and increases my productivity. However, outsourcing and delegating can increase your stress level, if you do not give clear instructions and set strict deadlines. This, too, has been my experience.

Learn to Say "No"

This is a tough one to practise but believe it or not, learning to say "no" is a major productivity, time management and stress reducing hack. You must learn to say no to activities that are of lower value that do not contribute greatly to your highest value tasks.

According to the Pareto Principle, only 20% of what you do contribute to 80% of your results. Make your yeses fewer and your nos more. Now if you are going to do this, be prepared for some backlash. Remember, if you want to reduce your stress and be more productive, less is more. You cannot attend every party or be there for everyone.

Use the Pareto Principle to identify the relationships, business activities, goals etc. which mean the most to you. Once you identify your yes activities, develop the courage to say no. From now on, ask yourself daily as Tracy teaches, "What is the most valuable use of my time right now?" This will keep you on track.

Try it and see if it will increase your output and reduce your stress. Check out Gary Ryan Blair's video on YouTube on "The Power of No" to help you in learning to say no.

Making Times of Rest a Priority

In the Creation story in Genesis, we are told that the Creator rested on the seventh day after completing His creative activity. If the Creator of the universe set that example, we need to follow suit. I was shocked to learn in productivity expert Michael Hyatt's book, *Unleashing Nature's Secret Weapon* that going on six hours of sleep or less reduces your function to the level of someone who is legally drunk.

There is a saying, "if you snooze, you lose," but according to Hyatt, those who "sleep at night, soar in the day." Skimping on sleep, says Hyatt, "impairs our mental performance, creates

7.2 Being Money Smart

fatigue, inability to focus, slows reaction times and much more... Sleep refreshes our emotional state and boosts our immune system" (2017, 5-7). The effects of sleeplessness are significant.

Lack of rest reduces innovation and productivity. Sometime ago, a friend of mine called me and expressed how tired she was and how much she was in need of rest. She reported that she had become forgetful and was suffering from fatigue. She could not think clearly anymore from being overworked. She, however, admired the fact that I take one day off to rest. I told her that was non-negotiable for me. I will not ruin my life by not taking time off to rest. Monday is my preferred day off, because I work on the weekends.

Creatives like me need to take time off to renew our creative energies. This need is not only for Creatives. Our bodies are like phones and computers; we need to recharge often. An article in the Harvard Business Review by Tony Shwartz on Productivity makes the case quite well:

> As every great athlete understands, the highest performance occurs when we balance work and effort with rest and renewal. The human body is hard-wired to pulse, and requires renewal at regular intervals not just physically, but also mentally and emotionally. Unfortunately, rest and renewal get no respect in the organizational world. Instead, most managers instinctively view those who seem to need time for rest and renewal as slackers. But what are the costs of working continuously? Do we think as clearly, creatively and strategically, or work as effectively with colleagues and clients, in the 10th or 12th or 14th hour of a workday devoid of real breaks, as you do in the 2nd or the 4th?

I am a believer in making rest a priority to reduce stress and increase productivity. To ensure that this happens, here is what I suggest. At the start of the year—or right now—set your days off or vacation times first and plan everything else around them. View these days and times as scared times or a reward and work towards them. Here is a formula shared by Brian Tracy in his book *Focal Point* to work out the rest-work balance ratio.

- **Take 1 day off from work**: spend time with family and on personal pursuit. Do not do work; read about work or work on computer. Let your brain recharge and rejuvenate from regular work.

- **Expand the time to 2 days and a full weekend over time**.

- **Plan 3 days' vacation every 3 months.**

- **Plan 2-week vacations with family every year**—reorder your life, so you have more time with family.

Now, here's to your productivity, better time management and reduced stress!

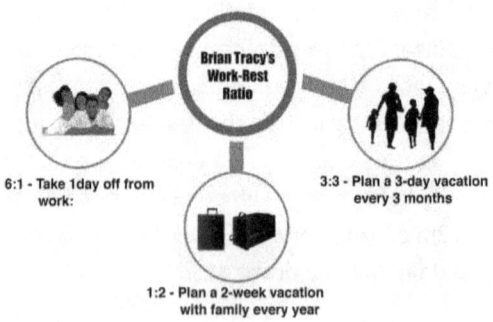

7.2
BEING MONEY SMART

There is a Bible proverb that says, "In the house of the wise are stores of choice food and oil, but a foolish man devours all he has" (Proverbs 21:20). Unfortunately, I was not financially wise in young adulthood but I am determined to become financially independent and retire early in the next season of my life.

Money management is an area in which many people struggle. This is an essential life skill that all of us should get right early on. Unfortunately, most of us were never directly taught this valuable skill.

Over and over the studies show that the majority of people are living from pay cheque to pay cheque. Jokes abound about our JOB (Just Over Broke) and the reality is: very often it's not that we don't make money, or have money pass through our fingers… it's just that it keeps passing through.

Either we don't know how to spend it, or we don't have enough of it. The problem is compounded even more in that, even if we mentally understand it, very often our behaviour is just the opposite.

It is for this reason that financial expert Dave Ramsey says, "Personal finances is 20% head knowledge and 80%

behaviour." Here are 10 keys to win with money which I have adapted from money experts to help you to win with money as you get older.

Ten Keys to Win with Money

1. **Become an excellent earner**: You cannot manage what you don't have. Study income generation. Aim for a minimum of three income streams, some passive and some active.

2. **Simplification:** Simplify your lifestyle so that you can live on less than you make.

3. **Track Your Money.** Know where it all goes. Live on a budget.

4. **Be an Excellent Manager**: What you don't manage well you lose/waste. Manage money God's way: God is the owner of everything. Management means having a system or plan that enables you to give, spend, save and invest.

5. **Dollar Assignment:** Separate your money and assign each amount to specific purposes.

6. **Become Generous:** Excel in the grace of giving. After taking care of yourself and family, this is the next goal. Always give to charity/God/church even if you are indebted. Many Christians use 10% of their income as a standard for giving.

7. **Pay Yourself First:** This means you save and invest before you spend. It does not matter the amount, save a portion before you spend.

8. **Expert Investment Advice:** Get proper investment advice from experts. Never invest in something you do not understand.

9. **Eliminate Debt as Much as Possible**: The borrower is slave to the lender. Debt hinders generosity.

10. **Build Wealth Legitimately but Don't Be a Rich Fool**: The rich fool is one who is wealthy materially but spiritually bankrupt and forfeits eternal life.

As we get older, we must be smarter with money. We must be intentional about getting out of debt and preparing for retirement. Your income is your greatest wealth building tool. If you do not earn, you cannot eat or pay your bills. If you are not earning, someone else is earning so you can live.

Earning does not necessarily mean having a 9-to-5 job or waiting on a salary at the end of the month, because even children can earn. It means finding a way to be compensated monetarily for your service.

Winning with money requires discipline, sacrifice and consistency with clear long-term goals in mind and the development of a plan. In this regard, I want to share a proven money-management system that has literally gotten millions of people out of debt and enabled many to become millionaires. I started using it and was able to clear over US$5000 in debt in a little over a year.

Dave Ramsey's Money Map

Dave Ramsey's story is one of riches to bankruptcy to riches again. In the early 1990s, Ramsey made some bad financial decisions and became heavily indebted. Ramsey had a young family, and during this time, he became a Christian and learnt principles from the Bible to manage his money. The main principle he learnt at that time was: "the borrower is slave to the lender." Dave, having experienced this personally, began to wage war on debt. Over the last 25 years, he has enabled millions of people to get out of debt through his book, *Total Money Makeover*, his *Financial Peace University* (a 9-week financial course) and "The Dave Ramsey Show."

Dave has succeeded in changing his financial family tree, and now one of his daughters has joined him in the war on debt. The Ramsey Show is a daily three-hour broadcast, which is aired on 500 radio stations in the USA, Canada and other countries.

7.2 Being Money Smart

Each week, he has a millionaire themed hour where millionaires share their journey. There is also an exciting "Debt Free Scream" segment, where persons who have gotten out of debt come to share their story and make their debt free scream.

These are truly exciting and inspiring initiatives which give people the hope of winning with money. Dave Ramsey's company Ramsey Solutions now employs over 400 people. He has truly turned tragedy into triumph, and now he teaches people to plan holistically for their financial success.

Ramsey teaches seven (7) "Baby Steps" which must be followed sequentially to eliminate debt and build wealth. However, steps 4-6 can be done together. They are as follows:

Baby Step 1: US$1,000 cash in a beginner emergency fund. Do whatever it takes to save this portion. This often means finding a way to earn more, getting a second job or selling things that are not absolutely needed. This should be done as quickly as possible. Doing this first prevents you from going back into debt for little emergencies and acts as a buffer.

Baby Step 2: Use the debt snowball to pay off all of your debt but the house. This means listing all debts from smallest to largest and attacking them in that order using income from your second job, other earning initiatives or sale of assets.

Baby Step 3: A fully funded emergency fund of 3 to 6 months of expenses.

Baby Step 4: Invest 15% of your household income into retirement.

Baby Step 5: Start saving for college.

Baby Step 6: Pay off your home early.

Baby Step 7: Build wealth and give generously.

Note well: Ramsey's plan calls for a simplification of your lifestyle and tremendous sacrifice. It means working hard and living on "rice and beans" until the debt is cleared.

This is why Ramsey's mantra is "Live Like No One Else." Investment should only be done after Baby Step 3. Ramsey's plan prohibits borrowing for anything except the purchase of a house.

If this plan does not suit you can create your own or modify it. What matters is having a plan and being disciplined to stick to it. Study how money works. In closing this segment, I am including some useful resource material to help you to win with money.

- *Total Money Makeover,* Dave Ramsey
- *The Millionaire Next Door,* Thomas J. Stanley and William D. Danko
- *Everyday Millionaires,* Chris Hogan
- *The Legacy Journey,* Dave Ramsey
- *Smart Money Smart Kids,* Dave Ramsey and Rachel Cruze
- *Retire Inspired,* Chris Hogan

7.3
CREDIT CARD ADVISORY

According to leadership expert Peter Drucker, "There is nothing so useless as doing efficiently that which should not be done at all." I could not close this book without doing a feature on credit cards. Credit card mismanagement has been one of my regrets, and I am educating as many persons as possible about the need to be careful with credit cards.

Total credit card debt has reached its highest point ever, surpassing $1 trillion in 2017, according to a separate report by the Federal Reserve of the United States. Credit card debt is one of the leading causes of bankruptcy.

My goal here is to briefly expose some of the hidden dangers of credit card fees which come with mismanagement, so that I can help you to become a better steward of a credit card or to eventually surrender the "need" for one.

Once you have a credit card and depending on how many you have, it can become burdensome. If you are only making minimum payments, you have just added a "utility bill" to your list of monthly expenses. You will have a recurring monthly fee, which if not paid will result in fines.

Sadly, unlike the electric company, cable company or water commission, credit card companies will not cut your service for non-payment. They will let the charges increase ad infinitum. In this regard, the credit card becomes a strict teacher in the school of discipline.

Having one or more credit cards is an excellent way to be schooled in the art of discipline: the discipline of paying attention to and monitoring your deadlines, and exercising control over your impulses.

Trust me, the pain of mismanagement will teach you how to be vigilant like no other teacher! When deadlines are missed, you are in trouble! And when you fail to keep your spending impulse in check, there will be "hell" to pay in fees: anxiety, depression, insomnia, hypertension and the like, and, sadly, bankruptcy and even suicide in some cases.

A credit card is a psychological trap. One of the reasons so many businesses are going cashless is that when you use a card, you do not feel it until the bill comes. When you spend hard cash, it is reported; this activates the pain centre in the brain, but paperless transactions like a credit card do not.

If you are not careful, you will purchase many little items online and elsewhere, and only when the bill comes do you feel the delayed pain.

In addition, the use of the card may prevent you from bargaining or negotiating for a lowered price or good deal. After all, who negotiates with a computer, card machine or Amazon online?

"Hidden" Fees

"Hidden" refers to fees you did not readily think of when you were getting the card or fees the credit card sales person never explained to you or highlighted. In many cases, the emphasis is

7.3 Credit Card Advisory

only on two payments: the minimum fee and the annual user fee.

Bear in mind that "fees" means money you are or may be liable to pay to the credit company. These fees in many cases do not decrease your principal loan nor need to be paid any time at all.

The only way to avoid most of these penalties is to make sure you pay the card in full on time each month and never lose the card. This is especially so if you have a card with an annual fee.

The following is a list of 15 possible credit card fees based on rates and charges in 2016 for a Mastercard. This information came in a brochure I received from the bank. Pay close attention to the percentages, and I will share a story about the implications. The results will shock you!

I am using my MasterCard as an example. However, other cards like Classic Keycard, Lovebird Keycard, Gold Keycard, Travel Mastercard, etc. have the same categories of charges though the amount varies.

1. *Primary Joining/Annual Fee*
2. *Supplementary Annual Fees*
3. *Replacement Card Fee*
4. *Annual Interest rate [Unsecured] – 18% -21%*
5. *Annual Interest rate [Secured] – 15%*
6. *Cash Advance Fee at NCB Branch – 10% plus GCT*
7. *Cash Advance Fee at ABM – 7.3% plus GCT*
8. *Over Limit Fee*
9. *Late Payment Fee*
10. *Returned Cheque*
11. *Replacement Statement*
12. *Credit Report [per report]*
13. *Credit Bureau Fee*

14. *Voucher Search/Item Retrieval—per item (at cardholder's request)*
15. *Monthly Minimum Payment –4% of monthly statement balance*

Tell the truth! If you already have a credit card, were you aware of all possible charges when you signed up? I sure was not! Furthermore, do you see the danger of #15, which is exactly how the bank wants you to make you a credit card slave?

Note Well: In Jamaica, we do not operate in US dollars. Each month, a Jamaican will pay a different amount based on the fluctuation of the Jamaican dollar upon conversion. You lose if your primary currency is not the same as the credit card.

Sam's Story

I will use Sam as an example to illustrate how these charges may affect you.

User Fee: Sam has a US Dollar MasterCard with a limit of $1000.00. Let's say he has had his card for 10 years and only paid the annual user fee. This means Sam either paid the card in full whenever he used it or he never used it.

If the user fee remains at $60.00 for 10 years, Sam has given the credit card company US$600 to retain/use the card. It is likely that the cost would have increased in those years as well.

What if Sam gave up the card in year three and had an emergency fund of US$1000? Sam would have saved at least US$420, which he could have invested elsewhere.

Now is it really worth it, Sam? No wonder Stephen Covey says effective people have the habit of starting with the end in mind. I say think long term to win!

7.3 Credit Card Advisory

Minimum Payments and Other Fees: Imagine Sam had a medical emergency and maxed out his card, and for some reason, he resorted to paying only the minimum payments for 10 years. He would automatically have been giving the credit card company more money.

4% of 1000 is 40; 40 x10 = 400

Now add the annual user fee of $600 for 10 years. In 10 years, Sam would have paid the credit card company at least US$1000, and his credit card principal would remain untouched.

He still owes them US$1000!

The situation is even more frightening if Sam missed payments, paid the minimum payment late during those years and made a cash advance/withdrawal. His balance would have increased, and he would have had to give more money to the bank than he originally borrowed.

By now, you get the point. Is it really worth it, Sam?

I have been Sam and there are many Sams out there! I hope that you are seeing the insanity of it all.

If you do need to have a credit card, bear in mind the responsibilities, and do not become a victim of stupid taxation through mismanagement.

Questions to Ponder

Having delineated the above, honestly answer the following questions:

    a)   Do you still want a credit card?

    b)   If so, are you only making minimum payments?

    b)   Have you been paying your credit card on time?

c) Do you have credit card regrets?

d) Is it worth keeping a credit card?

e) Can you really manage this responsibility?

f) Is there a better way to do your business without a credit card?

We have come to the end of our PAPA framework. I trust that these life-hurdling skills will help you to be more effective in your life as you grow older. I wish you joy and fulfilment as you apply them.

7.4
SPRING AGAIN

How long has it been since your dream has been delayed? How long has it been since your gift has been dormant? Perhaps like my Mom it's been over 30 years. Maybe like Colonel Sanders, you are in retirement or like Elizabeth and Zechariah at a very old age. But if the fire and desire are still there, it's time to spring again! It's time to shoot again!

The Banana Story

This idea of springing and shooting again emerged as I watched a fascinating tale of a banana tree over the summer of 2018. My connection with bananas in hindsight, go way back. I am from St. Mary, known as the banana parish in Jamaica. My grandmother worked on a banana plantation and I grew up with bananas. Even today, in Kingston, I am surrounded by banana trees in my backyard and my neighbours have banana trees.

Over the course of two months, a story unfolded that reignited my passion, courage and mission to empower people to win despite the odds. I observed a fallen bunch of bananas with about nine (9) lovely hands of bananas, and for some reason it caught my attention.

Banana trees are negatively geotropic. When they begin to bear fruit, they will lean and eventually topple under the weight of its fruit. If there is no support, the fruit may not come to maturity and thus its purpose will be aborted.

It appeared that the owner did not do a good job of supporting this banana tree and so it toppled, but not before bringing its fruit to maturity. After it toppled, I was invited to speak at a conference on mentoring and suddenly the banana tree started to "speak" to me.

If you have read my book, *When Trees Talk*, you will know how "messages" from trees have transformed my life and have given me tremendous insights about winning at life and career. I learnt five lessons from this banana saga.

Lesson 1: Be a Stick to Someone

The banana tree fell by the wayside because the stick supporting it fell. Who will fall by the wayside because there is no support? Who is in danger of not realizing their full potential because there is no stick (support) to give them the stability to thrive? I need to be a banana stick to others and raise up other banana sticks! As you get older, be a stick to the next generation.

Lesson 2: Don't Become a Rotten Banana

The next scene that unfolded was that after the banana tree fell, its fruit were left lying on the ground beaten by the sun and the rain for many days until eventually they rotted.

When I saw the rotted bananas, I cried. The banana tree delivered a powerful message. "You could have become a rotten banana." It's true. I could have become a rotten banana – useless and spoiled, had it not been for the people God used to give me a vision of His purpose for my life.

I could have ended up a rotten banana after my devastating relationship breakup at age 34, had it not been for a revelation of my Design to Win and the support from family, mentors and friends.

7.4 Spring Again

Had it not been for the intervention of some older persons when I was a teenager, through whom God revealed the picture of my purpose and my future, I would not be here today. God revealed how I would become fruitful and useful. Today, I am impacting lives around the world through my books, speaking and coaching.

Do not let your fruit die. Seek support. Ask God to reveal to you a design for your future so that the fruit in you will not rot. Get help from a coach or mentor.

Lesson 3: Raise Up Successors —Pass It On

While the fruit of the mother banana tree was rotting, the mother banana tree sent up a new shoot. The life cycle of a banana tree is nine (9) months but before it dies, it sends up a shoot. This spoke to me about the need for succession and legacy. Your gifts/business/ministry etc. must not die with you. Raise up others to continue these things.

Lesson 4: Spring Again Despite the Odds

After the bananas rotted, the owner cut down the mother tree and its shoot. When I saw that my heart sank. It seemed that there was no hope. Both the mother tree and its shoot appeared dead. But was I wrong?

Several weeks later the young shoot sprang again! I was so elated. That's a second chance I thought. The banana tree had gotten a second chance!

If you are alive today, you still have a chance to thrive. Spring again despite the odds!

Lesson 5: Don't Let Others Die Because of Your Fear

I realized that part of what happened was my fault. I had the vision of the usage and possibilities for the bananas. But I lacked the courage to ask the owner for the bananas.

Once again, the banana tree "spoke" to me and I was in tears. "Who will fall by the wayside or lose their second chance because you lack the courage and the willingness to help?"

I pledged that day to act with courage so that people will not become rotten bananas. I then mustered the courage to ask the owner for the next yield of bananas.

He, to my surprise, consented and now I look on with hope and expectancy for bananas. These bananas will become food for my stomach and maybe money in my pocket. I will also share them with others.

This book is your banana stick and framework to spring again so that you can become fruitful and useful as you grow older.

The winds and waves of life may have caused you to topple over. Some of your fruits may have rotted but you still have life and there is a chance you can shoot still before you die.

Let the banana tree be your dream resuscitation and life reinvention compass. It's time to send up a shoot or spring again like the banana tree.

Someone's destiny is tied to you. Someone's deliverance is tied to your goals and dreams, to your mission and purpose. Don't keep them waiting!

AFTERWORD: A DREAM REVIVED

At the time I began writing this book; one of my dreams (attaining my doctoral degree) had been lying dormant for three years. In 2014, after my broken engagement, I started looking for options to migrate and pursue doctoral study overseas.

After researching my options for school and possible scholarships, I started classes to prepare for my Grade Record Examination (GRE) to matriculate to a university. In the process, I depleted my emergency fund because I was not working, and I was transitioning after being a full-time missionary for four years.

One day while praying and reading Psalm 37, I felt redirected. I read a verse that said, "Live in the land, feed on truth and I will sustain you" (v.3 CEV). I immediately halted my plans for migration which meant I had wasted over J$200,000 (US$2000 at the time).

Nevertheless, I still continued to pursue the desire to do a doctoral program. I began searching for a program that I could do online without leaving Jamaica and without doing a GRE.

Eventually, I found a program at Bakke Graduate University. I enrolled and was accepted to start the program in 2015 but with all the turmoil in my life at the time, and poor financial state, I could not begin the program. Now both my dreams of marriage and my doctorate were once again delayed.

Years of Development

Over the next three years (2015-2018), I plunged myself into writing. I wrote four books and began helping others to publish theirs. I began doing workshops from my books and coaching others to win. My books created a platform for me to speak in different countries including South Africa and Uganda.

I was interviewed several times on radio, newspaper and on television. I became a career and personal development coach and developed a passion to empower youths. I launched my Design to Win Academy in May 2018 and became a full-time author-entrepreneur in July 2018.

During this period of change, I felt a stirring in my spirit to resume my doctoral studies. I was surprised and wondered how I would fund it and if this was truly God speaking or just my imagination.

Despite my apprehension, I obeyed the voice and contacted the school. It was then that something amazing happened! The school confirmed that my work as an Authorpreneur could become my doctoral dissertation. I also still qualified for a 30% scholarship.

I recognized then that the delay had equipped me for greater impact and was part of my development for this phase of my journey.

Repositioned

I now know that on our journey of life, delays are not always denials to our destination. They are but detours for development and re-routing for something better. In March 2019, I completed my first doctoral course and that single course transformed my life.

As I draw closer to 40, I am no longer dreading it. I am focusing on retiring right and being activated for greater things. I no longer feel unhappy about the dreams that have not yet been accomplished. My perspective has changed. The delays have repositioned me for greater.

I don't know your age or stage, but if your dreams have been delayed, it's not necessarily a denial. Now is the time to set a better sail! I urge you to re-read the dream resuscitation stories. Study the reinvention tips and use the PAPA Design to Win Framework to go after your dreams!

It's time to revive your dream and spring again! It's not over until you win!

ACKNOWLEDGMENTS

I give all praise and thanks to my King, Christ Jesus, who has been the God of all comfort, my wise counsellor and Design to Win Coach. Surely without His help, I would be nothing.

I am also grateful for the Bible and its truths which guided me every step of the way in putting this framework together.

To my immediate family, especially my mother, thanks for partnering with me on this journey! Mom, you are hands down the biggest supporter of my books. I pray that you will soon reap tangible rewards for your faith and investment over these years.

I am very grateful to my friends on Facebook who gave wise heartfelt responses to dealing with regret. Special thanks to Cynthia Pearson, Vaughn Tucker, Nordia Vassell, Nickell Bailey, Racquel Newman, Vena Morgan and others who took the time to respond.

Certainly, I cannot fail to thank Jo-Ann Richards-Goffe for your wonderful fore- word and encouragement over the years. Thanks for believing in me. It has been a joy to see you soar to new heights as you get older.

I am especially grateful to Rev. Mark Dawes, Grace-Ann Taylor-Myers, Claudette Distant-Lindo for allowing me to share their stories in this book. You have taught me not to give up on my relational dreams.

Thank you, Dr. Jean Lee, for editing this work. Special thanks to J.C. Hendee and the N.D. Author Services team for always responding so quickly to my publishing needs. Thank you for the cover design, and special thanks to Norman Cooper for the infographics.

Thanks to Kerone Edwards and other clients who trusted me to coach you with the Design to Win Road Map. Your results have been amazing and it has been a joy to see you achieve your dreams.

Finally, I am grateful to Rev. Carla Dunbar and all my late bloomer friends who continue to soar to new heights as you get older. You have been used by God to activate me for greater and lose my fear of getting older and not winning.

.

ABOUT THE AUTHOR

CAMEKA "RUTH" TAYLOR is an Authorpreneurship expert, credentialled Master Teacher and coach from the beautiful island of Jamaica. She has 20 years of experience in teaching from the Early Childhood to the Tertiary Level of the education system in Jamaica.

She's the author of 20 books including two Amazon bestsellers and the *Fearless 40 Series*. She makes a full-time living from her writing and publishing skills and the income streams they generate.

Ruth not only publishes her own books but has helped many Caribbean authors to make their publishing dreams a reality, by breaking down the price barrier to entry and simplifying the publishing process.

She is on a mission to ensure fewer books die in the minds of their authors, that more manuscripts become published legacies and precious lives are transformed with the turn of each page.

She is committed to helping more people in the Caribbean and the African Diaspora to write, publish and share our stories and expertise as well as declare God's glory among the nations.

Through the Authorpreneurship Academy, her books and resources, she teaches authors and leaders to create greater impact, income and influence with non-fiction books.

With over 17 years of speaking and travelling experience in 14 countries thus far, Ruth continues to activate, educate and empower thousands of people in Jamaica, countries in the wider Caribbean, Latin America and Africa to win in their personal, professional and spiritual lives for the glory of God.

Contact her at ruthtaylor@extramileja.com if you need her coaching, writing, publishing or speaking services. Visit her website www.extramileja.com/ to read her blogs and learn more about her endeavours.

Join her Authorpreneur Secrets Academy to get the training and tools to be activated for greater in writing, publishing and monetizing your book.

NOTE: Please don't forget to submit a book review wherever you bought this book online and send your feedback to the author. Thank you.

REFERENCES

Bolles, Richard. *What Colour is Your Parachute?* 2018 Edition. Ten Speed Press, 2018.

Covey, Stephen. *The 7 Habits of Highly Effective People*. Rosetta Book, 2013.

Duhigg, Charles. *The Power of Habits*. Random House, 2014.

Hyatt, Michael. *This is your Life Podcast*. Web. https://michaelhyatt.com/thisisyourlife

McCormack, Mark. *What they Don't Teach You in the Harvard Business School*. Bantam, 1986.

Munroe, Myles. *Overcoming Crisis*. Destiny Image, 2015.

Ramsey, Dave. *The Total Money Makeover*. Thomas Nelson, 2009.

Tracy, Brian. *Eat That Frog*. Berrett-Koehler Publishers, 2007.

---------------. *Reinvention*. AMACOM, 2009.

RESOURCES BY C. RUTH TAYLOR

Visit www.extramileja.com/home to get a free e-copy of her bestselling book *Design to Win Road Map, Youth and Millennial Edition* to equip youths to win at life.

If you are interested in Indie publishing, join our free Facebook tribe "Indie Authorpreneurs" to learn how to publish on a budget, create multiple income streams and impact more lives with books. Upon joining, you will get a 1-page pre-publishing checklist and other goodies.

Subscribe to Ruth's YouTube Channel to learn some Authorpreneur secrets and powerful, proven keys to win in your life and career.

Ruth's Fearless 40 Series

This is a series of seven books including *Design to Win Road Map 2, Late Bloomer's Edition* in celebration of Ruth's 40th birthday in May 2020. The series was birthed out of Ruth's own struggles to overcome feelings of regret and failure in certain key areas before age 40.

These books contain new perspectives on ageing and achievement. The books are designed to help persons who are approaching age 40, and those over 40 years of age to slay their fears/regrets and soar to new heights as they get older.

The books will inspire and equip you to go after your dreams, invest in the next generation and fearlessly chase your purpose even in your later years. See below the list of the other books in the series.

1. *Embracing Destiny: 21 Pep Talks to Walk in Your Greatness*

2. *Embracing Singleness: Secrets to Enjoy and Maximize It While It Lasts*

3. *Fearless 40: Getting Older, Slaying Your Fears and Soaring to New Heights*

4. *Pen It to Win It: Going Beyond Book Sales*

6. *Unshackled Queen: From Heartbreak to Wholeness*

7. *Write and Retire Right: Secrets to Write Non-Fiction Fast and Create Sustainable Income for Retirement*

You can find the series and several of Ruth's other books in her online bookshop at www.extramileja.com/ruthsbookshop, on Amazon and other digital publishing platforms. Get the *Fearless 40 Series* and tell your friends all about it.

www.ingramcontent.com/pod-product-compliance
Lightning Source LLC
Chambersburg PA
CBHW031645040426
42453CB00006B/212